Images of the Dance

Images
of the Dance

by

Richard Austin

Photographs by Carole Latimer

VISION

Vision Press Limited
11–14 Stanhope Mews West
London SW7 5RD

ISBN 0 85478 293 1

Printed in Great Britain
by Clarke, Doble & Brendon Ltd., Plymouth
MCMLXXV

For Natalia Makarova

. . . and though some said she played
I said that she had danced heart's truth.
W. B. Yeats

Contents

Acknowledgements

For permission to use copyright material, acknowledgements are made as follows: for quotations from *Burnt Norton, Little Gidding, The Hollow Men, Preludes* and *Rhapsody on a Windy Night*, from *Collected Poems 1909–1962* by T. S. Eliot, and from *On Poetry and Poets*, also by T. S. Eliot, to Faber and Faber Ltd; for the passage from "The Sunlight on the Garden" from *Collected Poems of Louis MacNeice*, to Faber and Faber Ltd; for a quotation from "Crazy Jane Grown Old Looks at the Dancers" from *The Collected Poems of W. B. Yeats* by permission of M. B. Yeats, Miss Anne Yeats, Macmillan of London and Basingstoke and Macmillan Co. of Canada; for the passages from *Ballet: Traditional to Modern* by Serge Lifar, to the Bodley Head; for quotations from *Great Morning* and *Laughter in the Next Room* by Osbert Sitwell, published by Macmillan, and for quotations from "Most Lovely Shade" and "Heart and Mind", from *Collected Poems* by Edith Sitwell, also published by Macmillan, to David Higham Associates Ltd. The translations from *Letters on Dancing and Ballets* by J. G. Noverre and from *Ballet: Traditional to Modern* by Serge Lifar are by Mr Cyril Beaumont.

I am also most grateful to Miss Hilary Tickner, Miss Susan Lockwood, Miss Jacqueline Elliott and Miss Lynn Hollamby, all dancers of The Royal Ballet, who posed with such enthusiasm and good humour for the photographs taken to illustrate this book. I owe a particular debt of gratitude to Miss Tickner who helped to arrange the photo calls and for the advice she gave me on technical matters in choosing these poses. These dancers were photographed by kind permission of Mr Kenneth MacMillan, Director of The Royal Ballet, and Mr Peter Wright, Associate Director, to whom I am also grateful for making a studio available at the Royal Opera House, Covent Garden.

I should also like to thank Miss Mary Scudamore for her translations of the various quotations from the writing of the late André Levinson; also for her help in reading the proofs and compiling the index.

Introduction

Inspired by the performances of one great ballerina to whom this book is dedicated, I found myself speculating more and more on the nature of the classical dance as she expressed it. This study is, therefore, more an investigation than a tightly-worked theory of aesthetics, a personal quest for the source of an art whose beginnings are lost in the darkness of an unknown world, and whose fulfilment is never finally achieved, or, if so, grasped only fleetingly at isolated moments during a performance.

As I studied the ballet, I found that little had been written in English to deal with the art in any fundamental way; most books are the expression of varying opinions about certain ballets and dancers, some of them, it is true, of considerable interest, but none seemed to study the nature of Ballet in terms of aesthetics, or in relationship to life and its sister art of poetry. It remained a specialist subject, with its own terminology and its own assumptions, such as the theories of Michel Fokine, that I found myself increasingly beginning to question.

In France the situation is different: the dance is seen, not in isolation, but in relationship with other arts, while a number of great poets, including Baudelaire, Mallarmé and Paul Valéry, have written about it with an understanding of its poetic truth that seems barely to have been grasped by professional ballet critics. I have, therefore, allowed the poets and dancers to lead the way (though not the male dancers in whom I have little interest) for their intuitive knowledge of the art is more valuable than the writing of any critic, whose creative abilities do not extend beyond the limited range of his own discipline.

I have made an exception by drawing extensively on the writings of André Levinson, because of their brilliant insights and the exquisite balance of his prose, a verbal equivalent to the classical dance itself.[1] Further, his devotion to that style and to the dancing of Anna Pavlova, who was its supreme exponent, is not dissimilar to my own attitude to the other "sublime vagabond" (as Levinson called Pavlova) of our own times.

But I have left the dancers to have the last word, as they had the first. They are the guardians of this ancient tradition, and their dancing its ultimate justification. I think it is fitting that this book should be illustrated by photographs taken in class of young dancers from the Royal Ballet, since the tradition of the art is continuous, and they are the most suitable representatives of a new generation to whom it has been entrusted. I can only follow them, in gratitude and admiration, knowing full well as their emissary that "the words of Mercury are harsh after the songs of Apollo".

[1] The original French texts of the quotations from André Levinson are given in an appendix at the end of the book.

1. In the Beginning

Before love or grief were spoken, they could have been danced. Ballet, as we know it today, is not some distant and esoteric art; it draws its source from the basis of human emotion as it was first formed in movement. The *pas de deux* in one of the great classical ballets bears the same relation to man's first gesture of love made at the dawn of time, as the sonnets of Shakespeare relate to his first words as they were shaped out of the stillness. The human spirit speaks today through the dance as it did in the primaeval light of the world. It is the language of our being, refined through the centuries, made accessible in a theatrical art that reaches to us in the images of the formal dance.

Ballet is the outward expression of our inner emotional life; of all arts it is the most accessible, as it deals in the primary emotions—in love, in grief, in betrayal and reconciliation, that are outside time and the changing of fashion, known to all types and conditions of men even beyond our history, as we know its first beginnings. Writing in A.D. 125, Lucian says: "It would seem that dancing came into being at the beginning of all things and was brought to light by Eros, that ancient one." As men first loved, so they danced—reaching towards one another in the same way as the ballerina and her partner stretch out their arms in greeting as their dance begins. One can see the *pas de deux* as a kind of mating dance, with its solemn walks, its coming together, its parting, its elaborate courtesy and sense of controlled passion. The classical ballet is not, therefore, a kind of pretty decoration, set in a tinselled fairyland; it is the expression of our most secret hearts.

There is little doubt that primitive man used the dance as a form of ritual in which he could express not only his own joys and griefs, but also a way of propitiating nature and the hostility of the gods. He could celebrate—at the coming of Spring, or at the fullness of Midsummer; he could terrify his enemies with tribal dances of great savagery; he could even disarm those he wished to conquer in the animal or spirit world by imitating them in his dance, so that they were assimilated into his own being and rendered powerless thereby.

It is probable that the magic rites of primitive man were among his first dances. The dance with its pounding rhythms, beaten out on a drum or similar instrument, began to take possession of him, so that he must have fallen into a kind of hypnotic trance in which, for a time, this weak and frightened creature, of all the animal kingdom in many ways the most powerless, felt that he was equal to the gods, gifted with a strength beyond all his fellows. This is not a state of which we today are entirely ignorant; to watch the stamping and gyrating of young people in a discotheque, dancing to the elementary rhythms of "pop music" is to understand how even today we seek to escape from our own savage gods—of poverty, loneliness and the fear of sudden death. The mass hysteria of "pop" festivals produces in the spectators a trance-like state that can be little different from those of primitive man, circling in fear and exultation his own different but no less powerful gods.

It is impossible to deny man his need to dance; if all our civilisation were to be carried away, some man in the unknown future would be seen to dance, even among the ashes of a dead star. To dance is as fundamental in human nature as to speak or sing. Before he can talk a child will dance with rage or with joy, will stamp or jump, retaining in his movements the shadow of those same dances of primitive man. It is likely that the first music known to man was made by himself clapping his hands or drumming his feet on the earth to accompany his dance. He made his own music, established the first counter-rhythms to add complexity to his steps, in much the same way as the

Spanish or Greek dances incorporate these primitive sounds within a context of far more sophisticated movement.

Traces of how men and women danced in the ancient world can be found in Egyptian carvings going back over six thousand years: in the frescos from the Minoan age in Crete, and in the sculptures and temple carvings of the Greek civilisation. No one knows what Grecian urn it was that inspired Keats' great Ode, but what he saw was a kind of dance:

> Fair youth, beneath the trees, thou canst not leave
> Thy song, nor ever can those trees be bare;
> Bold Lover, never, never canst thou kiss,
> Though winning near the goal—yet, do not grieve;
> She cannot fade, though those hast not thy bliss,
> For ever wilt thou love, and she be fair!

In Greek vases and friezes the dances of that civilisation are immortally preserved: they are full of movement, of what is called "line" in classical dancing, as if the dance had been caught at one moment and frozen there for ever, as one of the famous poses of the classical ballet is today preserved by photography and on film. This sense of movement, caught in stillness, is marvellously evoked by T. S. Eliot in *Burnt Norton*:

> . . . Only by the form, the pattern,
> Can words or music reach
> The stillness, as a Chinese jar still
> Moves perpetually in its stillness.

Some twentieth-century choreographers have attempted to recreate these dances of primitive man, as in *The Rite of Spring* to music by Stravinski, and in *Requiem Canticles* by Jerome Robbins that seems to have been inspired by the funeral dances of the Cretans; while Nijinsky in *L'Après-Midi d'un Faune* and Frederick Ashton in *Daphnis and Cloé* invoked the world of a lost golden age that is preserved in mosaics, vases and statuary of the civilisations of Greece and Rome.

One of the pioneers of the modern movement in the dance, Isadora Duncan, sought to re-create the steps and poses of the ancient Greek dances which were to be the basis of her own performances and that of her followers. It was not, however, the dances themselves that brought her such great fame and made her so profound an influence on the history of the dance, but her own beauty, personality and genius for movement.

Like the dances of primitive man, the dances of early Greece were both social and religious, either to invoke the gods or to strengthen the men in battle, such as the famous Pyrrhic dance that itself must have had many tribal forebears and an echo of which is still preserved in the Maori war dances today. The shift in emphasis within the dance as a magical or tribal rite to a form of entertainment in which the dancers were not emotionally involved, but sought to project the emotion contained in the dance itself, may first have been developed by the Chorus in the Greek Tragedies. They were the first *corps de ballet* and their dancing and ritualistic movements served both to comment upon the action and to provide a link between episodes, as do the *corps de ballet* today, not only in classic works like *Swan Lake* and *Giselle*, but in the modern works of Ashton, Tudor and MacMillan. They mark the divide between the primitive and the modern dance where the emotion is expressed outwardly to an audience. The Chorus were, in a sense, the first professional dancers.

At the same time, as man obtained a greater control over his environment and felt himself less threatened by primitive forces, one sees the first beginning of the folk-dance when dancing becomes a social and communal act. This was to provide the ballet, as it developed, with a new source of movement in much the same way as folk-songs and dances have been incorporated into the music of many composers, notably that of Mahler and Bartok. If the Chorus in Greek Tragedy created the first theatrical dances, the folk-dance provided it with some of its raw material.

The Roman civilisation took over much of the Greek culture, including its dances. These became more and more a form of entertainment from which developed the *pantomimi*, a combination of mime and movement. This seems to have borne little relationship to the odious modern form of entertainment known as the Pantomime; indeed it was more closely related to the circus, in that the performers were also jugglers, acrobats and clowns. From this entertainment was to grow the Commedia dell'Arte whose Harlequins and Columbines lived on over the centuries, finding perhaps their most beautiful setting of all in Michel Fokine's ballet, *Carnaval*, danced to Schumann's music, itself also inspired by these same immortal figures.

The decline of Rome led to the association of the dance with the public games; as the city sunk into decadence, so the dancers and their performances were condemned by St Augustine and the Fathers of the early Church. Indeed, in the year 300 at the Council of Elvira, it was decreed that no person having connection with the theatre would be allowed as a candidate for baptism. As with so many other pagan survivals, the early Church took the dance and transformed it to its own ends, so that the first miracle and mystery plays were performed, even as they survive into our own time in the Passion Play at Oberammergau.

It is interesting to note that many of the ritualistic gestures and movements of the early Church, even those accompanying the liturgy of the Mass, were actually taken over from the movements of the pagan pantomime; indeed the liturgy of the Roman Catholic Church today (though sadly truncated) is as formal and theatrical as any of the pagan dances from which it sprung.

One of the most curious manifestations of the dance occurred, it seems spontaneously, in the fourteenth century when there broke out over Europe a kind of dance madness. Whole groups of people gathered together and seemed to work themselves up into a kind of delirium or trance; one might have thought they were diabolically possessed, for they seemed quite out of control and at the mercy of forces they did not understand. Maybe the recent absurd manifestation of "streaking" among the youth of the United States is a pale reflection of this, and perhaps stems from the same desire to break free from a society that appears to oppress them.

It was with the Italian Renaissance that the arts and humanities were at last set free; from the Court entertainments of that time one can find the first beginnings of ballet as we know it today. The Italian Renaissance was the spring-time of

Europe, a huge awakening to the visible world when man broke free from the shadows that oppressed his spirit, astounded by the beauty and mystery of all that lay around him. Italy was at that time a conglomeration of city states, ruled over by Princes whose wealth was expended on lavish banquets and entertainments, for the organisation of which they called upon the services of the professional dancing-masters. A number of these were Jews, since it was one of the few professions open to them. It was these professionals who first began to codify movement and to work out an aesthetic of the dance. Among them was Domenico da Piacenza whose treatise *De arte saltandi et choreas ducendi* (On the Art of Dancing and conducting Dances) appeared early in the fifteenth century. He did not so much invent new dances, but rather produced a kind of manual, describing the dances already in existence. This showed that the art of court dancing was already at a considerable level of sophistication and was not, as has sometimes been thought, a new invention of the Renaissance Courts. Two further treatises, written by his Pupils, Antonio Cornazano and William the Jew, about fifty years later, showed that already the technique had been developed and enriched.

The entertainments of the Courts of the Renaissance Princes were normally banquets, and would seem to us to have been enormous cabaret performances in which dancers, singers and actors combined together to express a common theme, usually drawn from the world of mythology. If it could have symbolic references to the power and generosity of the Prince in question, and throw some doubt concerning the wealth or power of a rival ruler, so much the better. A curious feature, in the largest of such entertainments, was the fact that a separate theme was served up, as it were, with each course, so that the fish might arrive to the accompaniment of a pageant of Neptune or the goddesses of the sea. A record has come down to us of one of the greatest of these given by Bergonzio di Botta in honour of the Duke of Milan and his wife, Isabella of Aragon, at Tortona in 1489.

The history of ballet is the story of the merging of different cultures and national styles of dance that has made it, of all arts, the most international, finding within the steps of the dance its only common language. The first such merger, that was to have a profound influence on its future development, came when, largely through the efforts of Catherine de Medici, the Italian style of entertainment and the Italian producers and dancing-masters were imported into France. The entertainment was in fact the merger of two distinct styles—that of the Italian courts and of the recently formed Académie de Musique et de Poésie in France. The resultant ballet, the *Balet Comique de la Royne*, performed in 1581 to celebrate the marriage between the Duc de Joyeuse and Marguerite of Lorraine, is often considered by historians to be the first Ballet. The choreographer (as one would describe him today) was an Italian Court musician, Baldassarino de Belgiojoso, whose name was altered by the French into Balthazar de Beaujoyeulx. He has an honoured place in the history of the dance, and is the prototype of all those guest artists, both dancers and choreographers, who have moved between different countries and enriched the tradition of ballet, and whose successors continue this process today.

It is at this point that the history of the ballet properly begins, and I shall take the story no further, as it has been told many times, notably in Ivor Guest's brilliant book, *The Dancer's Heritage*. Instead, I want, if possible, to try and construct an aesthetics of the dance, and to see this at work within the great ballerinas, whose art gives light and meaning to the whole.

2. The Ordering of Truth

"Beauty is the splendour of order." This remark by St Augustine reaches to the heart of the mystery of the classical dance. For the dance might be considered foremost as the ordering of human emotion within a formal design. In this way it belongs to the same world as poetry and music, as it does also to the sister arts of sculpture and painting. The ballet is, therefore, a synthesis of a number of different mediums, each expressive of a common emotion; and this synthesis, while it is made up of varying elements, produces an unique art that is a new thing and not just a close harmony of divergent forms. It is, as the great critic André Levinson has said, "one of the most stupendous discoveries of theatrical art".

All life is rhythmic. It is the pulse in our blood, our breathing, the underlying element of nature. It is seen in the movements of the seasons, the passing of day and night, in the whole vast rhythm of a transient world. We take this for granted, in the same manner as we are unaware of our breathing or the gestures we make, large and small, at every moment of our lives. Yet the complex muscular balance of the human body that makes all these infinitesimal adjustments to daily living, whether in terms of balance when we are stepping onto a 'bus, or in our spontaneous reaction to our feelings or the feelings of others, many of which we are barely aware, is a kind of dance. Indeed modern psychologists have now developed the science of what they call "body language" as if it were a new thing, but, in fact, when dancers make the arms "speak" they are merely controlling consciously an unconscious human mechanism. In the joyous ballets of Léonide Massine, for example, the dancer is often caught in a pose when both arms or shoulders are raised in merriment, and this is indeed a refinement of a gesture we have used a thousand times, whether we just shrug our shoulders, or throw our hands up in disgust or amusement.

To dance was man's first reaction to the visible world, since movement is the first response to nature. If a lion approaches, you do not analyse its movements, or try and draw it—you run. This may well have been the form of the first dance, fairly simple in its choreography, but certainly expressive of emotion. One is able to trace the ancestry of the classical dance back to such fundamentals and to see its vocabulary of turns and leaps and poses as highly refined versions of basic movement. This is important, for classical ballet is often attacked for being un-natural and artificial, when in fact the movements are merely stylized, abbreviated or compressed. It is the achievement of the greatest classical dancers that they are able to make one see the dance reaching beyond technique towards such fundamental expressions of behaviour. A young man who takes his girl's hand in the cinema performs a kind of dance, exactly as it is seen in the *rose adagio* of the *Sleeping Beauty*: the first action is spontaneous, the second formal; this is not a weakness in the classical dance, but its strength, in that it has refined movement to its basis, while still relating this to the outside world. A *pas de deux* is only a stylized version of a human encounter, either in love, antagonism or grief, so that it reaches the spectator directly; it speaks a common language, more basic even than the commerce of words.

But as well as an expression of our inner nature, we can see the dance also as moving outwards from the dancer; round her it spreads in infinite concentric circles, until it takes part in vast rhythms, from the moving of the winds, to the sea breaking on the shore. This is an idea that goes back to ancient times: Plato tells us that the Egyptian temple dances, one of the first dances of which we have any record, were expressive of the great harmony of the universe in which the planets and the stars move within an endless dance round the sun. The Fathers of the early

Church took over this idea and fixed it within the Christian ethos, when the dance is seen as the celebration of the Angels in heaven, where adoration and joy are expressed in movement. Basilius, who was bishop of Caesarea in the fourth century, expresses this idea when he writes: "We remember those who now, together with the Angels, dance the dance of the Angels around God, just as in the flesh they performed a spiritual dance of life and, here on earth, a heavenly dance."

In the design of the classical dance we see these rhythms compressed into images that are, at once, highly formal yet at one with nature. A *grand jeté*, for example, is both an academic step, having its own rules as to its shaping on the air, but it is also related to the movement of the clouds, or the breaking of a wave. At the same time it is one of the most basic of all human movements, even to a child's first leap of joy or rage. The technique of the classical ballet is thus a kind of shorthand in which is drawn the huge rhythms of human life. All is, in both a natural and theological sense, a dance, from the trembling of a leaf to the vast cosmic design of creation when the Spirit first brooded over the waters. In the natural sense, this is very well expressed by Sir John Davies in his famous poem *The Praise of Dancing* when he writes:

> For what are breath, speeches, echoes, music, winds,
> But dancings of the air, in sundry kinds?
> For when you breathe, the air in order moves,
>   Now in, now out, in time and measured true,
> And when you speak, so well she dancing loves,
>   That doubling oft and oft redoubling new
>   With thousand forms she doth herself endue;
>   For all the words that from your lips repair
>   Are nought but tricks and turnings of the air.

The dance as a theological concept is beyond human understanding, but we gain at moments hints of this when we feel the whole of creation dances to a Divine rhythm—from the circling of the planets, to the movement of an ant crawling across the earth—and that they relate, are part of a whole, aspects of a huge logic in the ordering of the world. All is one, the expression of a single Will. In the mystical writings of Julian of Norwich,

St John of the Cross and St Teresa of Avila, we obtain some insight into that reality; and it can also be sensed in certain of the greatest compositions of the dance that I shall deal with later.

The profound beauty of the classical dance resides in the fact that its movements are not expressive of a single aspect of life or emotion, but contain within themselves a whole series of associations. An outward gesture of the arms is at once an approach to another, a greeting; at the same time it is an image of the emotion contained within such a greeting, and it is also a shaping of that particular phrase of music on the air. Further it might be like the curve of a wave, or a sketch of a bird in flight, arched on sweeping wings. It can be all these things together, creating a relationship not just between two persons, but between them and aspects of the natural world. The dance is symbolic, an allegory of our being, an expression of the unity in nature. Its symbols are able to speak to us of the most profound truths, as, for example, in Ivanov's choreography for the Second Act of *Swan Lake* when Odette is presented as a magical creature, half woman, half bird, whose human nature is drawn from its disguise by the power of love. One does not have to look very far before one realises how profound an allegory that is of the growth and redemption of mankind through the power of love—a reality of both the human and the mystical world. It is with such immensities that the ballet is, of all arts, the most fitted to deal. It is not just a trivial form of recreation, though often it has in its history degenerated to this; its task is the ordering of truth within a formal style that is both its end and its beginning, and it is in search of this truth that all dancers take the stage.

3. The Divine Game

There is a sense in which the ballet is a form of play, one more subtle and sophisticated than any of the games of childhood, but with something of the same freedom and innocence. Indeed André Levinson has called it "un jeu divin". The Germans also have a word for it—*Spieltrieb*: the impulse to play, and one can see how closely this is related to theatrical art in the manner we speak of a certain actor "playing" a role. In a superficial sense there have been a number of ballets about games, including Nijinsky's *Jeux*, but one is looking for a deeper meaning than this. Otherwise one may go astray, rather like a newspaper critic reviewing Christopher Bruce's *Unfamiliar Playground*, who got the impression that the tubular scaffolding of the *décor* represented goal-posts!

This sense of play is clearly evident in the work of certain choreographers, notably Frederick Ashton and Jerome Robbins. The first scene of Ashton's *Daphnis and Cloé* depicts men and women who might, because of the neutrality of their costumes, belong to any period of our history, perform dances together with very simple lines that have something of the chaste elegance of a Grecian frieze. The ballet is set in the first light of the world, at once timeless and belonging to the early Greek civilisation, and it is pervaded with this sense of the innocence and wonder of untroubled childhood; it is an idealisation, that Gautier would have loved, of youth and the freedom of young people playing on some immortal shore.

The same atmosphere belongs to Jerome Robbins' *Dances at*

a Gathering, though here the ballet darkens towards its close and ends in a mood of quiet resignation, in the knowledge that youth and the games of youth will soon be over. It has in it, however, a kind of innocence, a kind of ardour, where the dances are performed almost like improvisations, carrying with them at times a sense of regret at the passing of youth and love—the shadows of evening that darken even the brightest day. The ballet opens with a male dancer wandering across the empty stage, lost in his own reveries; then he catches the first hint of the music and dances his first hesitant steps, so that one gets a sense of the loneliness and the impulsiveness of youth, caught by every breeze, the hint of music it carries on the air. It is a ballet about the games of youth—of flirtatiousness, rivalry and humour—that are to be interrupted only by the darkening of the sky and the sight of something terrible moving across the horizon that makes them wonder, makes them afraid. One does not have to know what it is they see; but they are changed by it, and the long day is over.

> Golden lads and girls all must,
> As chimney-sweepers, come to dust.

Writing about the nature of play, John Huisinga, in *Homo Ludens*, makes this important point when he defines play as "an activity which proceeds within certain limits of time and space, in a visible order, according to rules freely accepted, and outside the sphere of necessity or material utility. The play-mood is one of rapture and enthusiasm and is sacred and festive in accordance with the occasion. A feeling of exhaltation and tension accompanies the action, mirth and relaxation follow."

How apposite is this to the world of ballet and the two ballets I have described—the one sacred, since it takes place before the temple of Pan, and is concerned with the invocation of that deity; the other festive, a celebration of youth and love. Ballet takes place within limits of time and the space of the stage, and it is ordered by the technical rules of the classical style, the convention of which is "freely accepted" by the audience, while it is an art that has no relationship with utility. Indeed the essence of an art, it seems to me, is that it should have no purpose or moral value outside itself, other than to heighten our awareness of the beauty and strangeness of living.

In one of his earliest and finest ballets, *Solitaire*, Kenneth MacMillan shows us a very similar world of play, but here there is an outsider—the girl who wishes to join in every game, and is either ignored or excluded. *Solitaire* is primarily about loneliness, invoked at once in the sad, opening tune on the oboe. When the girl is invited by the others to join the game at the beginning of the ballet she does not at first think the invitation is for her; she glances behind her to see who it is they are calling. It is a most touching moment, a sudden insight into human nature that is both true and sadly revealing. Yet it is all a game, even though, like many of the games of youth, a cruel one. Later in the ballet the second female soloist dances a brilliant solo as a kind of sophisticated vamp, but it is made clear in the choreography that this is a game also; it is the fake, rather abashed sophistication of a child. The link between *Solitaire* and *Dances at a Gathering* is a very strong one; like the plays of Chekov, sadness lies below the surface of our laughter.

The mood in a number of MacMillan's ballets is one of quirkiness and a casual, unexpected wit. These are the games of ingenuity and daring, a kind of exploration of life and the oddities of living; they are, for the dancers, an experiment in which they rejoice at their new-found cleverness. One sometimes still hears the description of a child that "he is clever as a monkey", and it is this sense of playing with life that is part of many of MacMillan's ballets. In *Danses Concertantes* the dancers play games with the classical style itself, taking it apart like a new toy, treating it with the irreverence of the very young. It is not parody, but more subtle than this; it is more a kind of teasing, a lack of solemnity in taking up their inheritance as classical dancers. To mock anything, one must care about it, as these dancers care about their art. But it is something to be freely improvised, as in the games of childhood when grave matters of war and human aggression are fought over with wooden swords.

It is generally in his early ballets that a choreographer plays in this way with his ideas; there comes a moment when he shows us how these games conflict with the realities of living. For MacMillan, I think this was with his ballet *The Invitation*, in which the rape of a boy and girl by a much older couple shatters their youth beyond repair. For her, she can probably never love again; for him, he has lost for ever the innocence and daring of adolescence. For both, life is a game no longer.

It may well be that in his later years a choreographer will look back again on the games of youth, as did Robbins in *Dances at a Gathering*, but the tone of his ballets is likely to be different, eloquent of the brevity of life, the short time that remains, more nostalgic, and touched by certain sad remembrances. It is interesting that an early work of Robbins, *The Age of Anxiety*, based on W. H. Auden's poem, was as solemn, obscure and portentous a work as one can imagine, a study in collective *angst* without a glimmer of humour or daring. It lacked completely the brilliant inventiveness and high good humour of his ballet about three sailors on leave, *Fancy Free*; in it one sensed the intellectual solemnity about life that is one of the drearier products of American art, an age away indeed from the world of *Dances at a Gathering*. The ballet did not survive as its successor will, so deeply is it loved by audiences and dancers. I think it was a poor work because it had, within it, no element of play; it developed instead a social conscience which is, on the whole and with the odd exception like Jooss's *The Green Table*, the kiss of death to the ballet which deals with reality on an entirely different level.

Frederick Ashton's early ballets are explicitly about play: *Les Patineurs* is concerned with an afternoon and evening on the skating rink, *Les Rendezvous* with a series of light-hearted flirtations in a park. Like MacMillan he also reached a point in his creativity when he realised that the games can be shattered by reality: in his case in *Nocturne*, the story of an innocent flower girl betrayed by her rich admirer, where the sentimentality latent in such a theme is avoided by the impassive spectator (a role first played by Ashton himself) whose presence is a sad comment on the action, made more poignant by his inability to help the girl in her anguish.

Ashton's later ballets, however, returned to the world of make-believe after a creative span that included the expressionist *Dante Sonata*, composed during the war years to convey the anguish of that time. Maturity as an artist had brought him the same serenity that is to be found in Jerome Robbins' *Dances at a Gathering*, and this is most evident in *The Two Pigeons*, created in 1961. Here he presents us with a game of love, wistful, evocative and child-like, in which, like the two pigeons that flutter across the stage, his two lovers are sweetly reconciled to one another. In the gentle *pas de deux* between the young painter and his girl, he imitates in their movements the preening and fluttering wings of the pigeons, so that the atmosphere of make-believe is accentuated. In the girl's small beaten steps one is reminded of Valéry's delightful simile when he compares a dancer's feet to two doves quarrelling over a patch of grain. The element of play in this ballet is also present in the fact that it is entirely predictable; one never doubts from the first moment that the young man will be enticed away from his beloved by the Gipsy, nor that he will return; it has all the sense of reassurance that children demand from their games, where virtue and courage will triumph in the end.

If ballet, like play, has its own strict rules and conventions, much of its humour is achieved when these conventions are deliberately flouted. It gives the audience a sense of shock and amusement, but no feeling of unease, since these distortions of classical movement pre-assume the validity of the classical style. For example, in John Cranko's *The Taming of the Shrew*, a delightful effect is obtained when the three suitors of Bianca all dance together a series of *entrechats* with the toes pointing outwards instead of downwards to the stage; in the same way Katherine's waddling walk and upturned feet are a kind of parody of the ballerina's classical style. Ashton made the same joke in the Polka of *Façade*, where the ballerina proceeds to remove her ballet-skirt and reveal herself in corset and bloomers.

Audiences are flattered and reassured when the choreographer demands from them some specialised knowledge of the art. They feel at home, secure, like a child welcomed into a closed circle of friends who take it for granted he knows the rules of their game. Thus in Roland Petit's *Ballabile* a great deal of coterie fun was provided when the dancers imitated the dance of the four little Swans in *Swan Lake*, scratching at the ground like a lot of flustered hens. Similarly in *A Wedding Bouquet*, Ashton mimics the classical *pas de deux* in that between the Bride and the Bridegroom, during which, at one moment, he tucks her under his arm like a badly wrapped parcel. Such mimicry also occurs in the *pas de deux* between Alain and Lise in *La Fille Mal Gardée* when he seeks, in the classical style, to match her line, but with his arms stabbed wildly into the air and at the wrong moment, so that it appears more like a distress signal than anything else.

A related comic effect to this is when the choreographer arranges for men to imitate female movement, or to interchange their very different types of movement within the same ballet. Cranko in *Jeu de Cartes* provides us with the spectacle of the male dancer donning a skirt and performing like a rather drunken ballerina, while van Manen in *Septet Extra* achieves the most brilliant and startling effects when the men perform female steps and vice versa, to create a series of strange ambiguities in the dance.

But in all these ballets, the principle of the game is maintained: the style is fixed, the area of the stage is defined and limited, either by the scenery or by the *corps de ballet* who determine the space available to the solo artists, and the conventions are observed. When nudity has been introduced into the ballet, both by the Nederlands Dans Theater and the Royal Danish Ballet, it has failed to make any impact, either in the way of beauty (as Isadora Duncan maintained that it would) or in its power to shock. Stage nudity defies a convention by allowing realism into theatrical art, and paradoxically deadens its impact. The banalities of every day have no place in the ballet, as Gautier so often proclaimed: a naked girl is just such an intrusion, since it looks as if she has wandered onto the stage when looking for the showers.

By emphasizing the element of play in the ballet, one does not minimise it as a work of art, since all art partakes, at an unconscious level, in many of the aspects of play. But it is also an art that, by its refinement and the symbolic force of its language, is able to reach the most profound levels of human experience, as I have attempted to show in the preceeding chapter. It achieves its climax and its highest form of expression in the *pas de deux*, where "le jeu divin" becomes also the most sublime expression of human love and the mystery of human relations that the world of art has yet discovered. It is the heart of the classical dance.

4. Pas de deux

The *pas de deux* is a relationship in nature, between a man and a woman; in line and balance, between two bodies; in music, the reconciliation of harmonies. As music has in it both masculine and feminine principles—the one assertive, the other yielding—that are the basis of the classic symphonies of Mozart and Beethoven, so these are marked by the coming together of two different styles of the dance, each essential to the orchestration of movement. Sonata form is not an artificial device, but an expression of this dualism not only between the sexes but within our own nature, and it is this central truth that is explored in the *pas de deux*. The contrasting states are displayed singly in the two *variations* in the same manner as the two themes in sonata form are presented during the exposition. These unite in the *pas de deux*, as the themes are united within the development section of classical music.

The dancers are thus set in counterpoint against one another, where the female movements state the melody and the male the equivalent of the bass or accompaniment, rather in the same manner as in Chopin's piano pieces when the left hand provides the support for the theme played by the right. As we speak of a musical figure, shaped above the voice of the orchestra in a concerto, so we are dealing with the same image when in a *lift* the ballerina is carried by her partner, to be held often high in the air above him, to provide a visual figure designed in space. The images of the classical dance must be seen thus as aspects of music where the same principles of design, harmony and balance apply. Indeed Matisse, a painter with a profound understanding of the dance, has affirmed that "the *arabesque* organises itself like music, and it has its own particular tone". It is therefore necessary to study the images of the dance as musical forms and the music that accompanies it as visual images and see them thus together, so that the dance is simultaneously a visual and aural experience whose forms are interchanged between the two elements. It then provides an aesthetic delight of great intensity, where the emotion contained either in the situation or the dance is apprehended in two different but closely related (and inter-related) mediums. It may well be argued, indeed, that the synthesis of these two elements provides a new means of apprehension for which no existing visual or aural equivalent can be applied.

The early beginnings of the art of ballet in the Court dances of the reign of Louis XIV survive in the solemn walks, the formal approach of the dancers to one another, in the *pas de deux*. Indeed we emphasise this derivation when we speak of their courtesy, extending the word to designate an attitude of mind and behaviour. The man will bow, the ballerina will return his greeting; the tone is both elaborate and distant, but it is also an idealisation of the approach of the sexes to each other. The man is there to show off her beauty, add to her line, give her strength and support; in a sense it is he who displays the ballerina to her audience, a charming equivalent to the modern young man introducing his girl friend to his companions. The *pas de deux* is therefore not purely a matter of form, a study in line and balance, it is also the presentation of a relationship, idealised but not distorted, in human terms.

This relationship can, of course, be displayed in many different ways. It can be frankly erotic, as in the *pas de deux* between the Prodigal and the Siren in Balanchine's *The Prodigal Son*, where her scarlet cloak is used as a sexual symbol in exactly (though less explicit a manner) as a scarf or a fan is used by a strip-tease dancer to enhance her sexuality. The superb duet between himself and Renée Jeanmaire created by Roland Petit in *Carmen* is also openly erotic, though handled with perfect judgement and taste. Far more frequent is the use of the *pas de deux* as an expression of romantic love, as in Jerome Robbins' *In the Night*, where the succeeding dances are made to denote different stages of loving within a series of encounters that grow both more complex and more difficult to sustain, until the final reconciliation after a period of conflict, indeed of emotional antagonism, is achieved in the last *pas de deux*. The solitude and the exclusiveness of mutual love is also hinted at when the couples finally meet one another and the spell of their secret lives is for a moment broken. This is a beautiful insight, since every pair of lovers believe they are the only lovers in the world, that never until this time had such love been.

In Hans van Manen's brilliant small ballet *Twilight*, the relationship is brutally hostile—fierce, possessive and ultimately sterile, set in the urban jungle where such attraction is so often found in its bleak, disfigured streets. Here is a dance equivalent of T. S. Eliot's "Preludes" or his "Rhapsody on a Winter Night":

> You dozed, and watched the night revealing
> The thousand sordid images
> Of which your soul was constituted;
> They flickered against the ceiling.
> And when all the world came back
> And the light crept up between the shutters
> And you heard the sparrows in the gutters,
> You had such a vision of the street
> As the street hardly understands . . .

In van Manen's superb ballet, *Tilt* one sees the same world; as the couples enter to Stravinski's wry, sardonic waltz, they are touched for a moment by the kind of fake and ultimately sad glamour of the cheap night-club or dance-hall, where the music and the lights deaden the senses to the snatched embrace, the kiss wearily given in the cold lamplight under an urban dawn.

One of the greatest masters of the *pas de deux* was Michel Fokine in whose ballets they were used to explore highly complex relationships, going far beyond the traditional love duet that had been established since the nineteenth century. In *Petrouchka* the *pas de deux* between the Ballerina and the Blackamoor is an extraordinary study of the contrast between brute

B

force and callous indifference that leads to no final resolution. In *The Firebird* he created movements for the ballerina, as she struggles to free herself from the Tsarevich's embrace, that are harsh and jagged as a leaping flame. This is a world away from the duets between Harlequin and Columbine in *Carnaval* where the frail and brittle choreography, so full of mischief and inventiveness, has a kind of porcelain delicacy that is entirely appropriate to these immortal figures of the Commedia dell'Arte. In *Les Sylphides* the *pas de deux* is so ethereal that the ballerina drifts into and away from her partner's arms like a swirl of the night mist. Here the dance is composed of a series of fleeting images like glimpses within a dream. This type of Romanticism looks back to the nineteenth century and the ballets of long ago, when Théophile Gautier described their music "above which the ballet hovers like a dream to explain it".

No art can depict so directly as the classical dance the great human mysteries from the first awakening of love to the movement of the stars. A *pas de deux* can be intimate, as in so many ballets by Frederick Ashton, where it is like a whispered conversation, the secret encounter of two hearts; yet it can also convey the huge and cosmic truths about our world, a sublime example of which is the opening duet in Glen Tetley's *Voluntaries*, danced to the *Concerto for Organ, Strings and Percussion* by Poulenc.

It begins in silence, when the dancers seem to emerge from the primal dark in a world before time, in the great quiet before the moment of creation. The ballerina is poised with arms curved towards us like wings; the man stands behind her, to make a reference to the ancient myth where the woman was made from man's own being. Then a huge chord on the organ thunders out, shattering the stillness. It is as if, at one instant, the stars and moon leaped into the untenanted sky, the great forests grew their mortal leaves, and the first waves broke on the empty shore. Set thus, this opening *pas de deux* is a vision of glory, the Divine joy at the beginning of all creation. In this ecstatic dance one is reminded of the famous lines of Traherne in *Centuries of Meditation*:

The corn was orient and immortal wheat, which never should be reaped, nor was ever sown. I thought it had stood from everlasting to everlasting. The dust and stones of the street were as precious as gold: the gates were at first the end of the world ... And young men glittering and sparkling Angels, and maids strange seraphic pieces of life and beauty. Boys and girls tumbling in the street, and playing, were moving jewels. I knew not that they were born and should die; But all things abided eternally as they were in their proper places. Eternity was manifest in the Light of the Day, and something infinite beyond everything appeared: which talked with my expectation and moved with my joy.

This mystery seems at the base of Kenneth MacMillan's ballet *Concerto*, where the second movement is entirely composed as a *pas de deux* in which, in Natalia Makarova's interpretation, the ballerina experiences the slow growth of consciousness, the realisation, through movement, of her own being. Here we see her search from within an elemental darkness. She invokes the awakening of the human spirit, the first gestures that began to speak in human terms, to reach for the first time towards another in slow understanding. So, testing with her arms the unfamiliar air, as they grope, tendril-like, towards the light in the hushed stillness of this dawn, she shows us the dance as a primal act, made at the beginning of time. It grows almost organically out of the music, like a plant from the earth; it flowers and proliferates in a way that is totally natural, a part of nature. As the sun brightens (for the designers of both these ballets have used the same image of a patch of light spreading across the backcloth to provide a further symbol of human awakening) we find in her movements the stirring of inchoate being as the Spirit gave it form. We see these steps and poses take on a new mystery. One is made aware of an inner drama during which she explores their meaning, so that we recognise them as her first consciousness of her own identity, apprehended in physical sensation which she learns like a new language.

In his remarkable ballet, *Wings*, Christopher Bruce takes us back further, beyond consciousness, to our evolutionary beginnings. In this cold, unlit world primitive winged creatures hover, dimly knowing, within the instinctive dark. Between the sexes there is no contact: the females are swift, shimmering and rapacious; the males, heavy and full of menace, reaching towards one another with a glimmer of understanding, so that between two of them the first human contact is momentarily achieved. Here the music by Bob Downes, that echoes like the wind blowing around the still dead stars, is wonderfully effective. It rings hollowly in the void, in the emptiness of an unpeopled earth. *Wings* is a strange and beautiful work, icy and unfeeling, remote as the scarred face of the moon.

In creations such as these, one can see that a purely "abstract" ballet is a contradiction in terms, since it is a composition dependent upon the relationship between men and women. In Hans van Manen's majestic *pas de deux* to the slow movement of Beethoven's *Hammerklavier* Sonata, the dance is expressed in the most pure and abstract terms, yet a relationship between the dancers is present to which the choreographer draws our attention by the sudden glances they give to one another, as if to confirm the meaning they had found in this dance in each other's eyes. It is a beautiful invention to stress thus the human element within a formal design.

I do not wish to suggest that the classical *pas de deux* exists always at such sublime levels, nor that the dance-drama, as evolved by Fokine and Antony Tudor, cannot reach such heights, but I feel that the influence of Balanchine has been pervasive and is dangerous to the future of ballet if choreographers come to share his belief in the impersonality of the dance. The dancers cannot, for the health of the art, be allowed to degenerate into notes of music, a kind of visible architecture of the score that has become entirely dominant. They are human beings, not puppets, and they exist, the moment they enter the stage, in a relationship to one another, and from this relationship the great allegories of the classical ballet are devised.

5. The Art of Dreams

Every dream is, in a sense, a work of art. It is man's own private ballet in which are prefigured in symbolic form the doubts, fears and aspirations of his life. Often in the most fantastical costumes, or concealed under different, shifting forms, his deepest and most secret phantasies take the stage of his own dreaming; a performance out of time, given for him alone, is enacted every night. And not his dreams only, but fragments from the most ancient dreams of humanity that are preserved in his own subconscious, are invoked in the silence, in the darkness, as he sleeps.

In the same way, the dancers in a ballet are figures from a dream also, speaking a truth beyond the capacity of ordinary words, one that is both universal and unique to each person in the audience. There is a reality beyond language that is explored only by music and in the dance. It is the essential truth about our own emotions, created in such a form that its images reach directly to the subconscious, without the need for rationalisation, to be assimilated into the symbolic life hidden there. The images of the dance speak to it in the same language; they have not to be translated into words.

In the beginning was not the word, but the dance. Words deal with the appearance of things; they are a translation of the image into its approximate form, and by this translation the reality of the emotion they express is weakened and dissipated. The highest form of speech is poetry, since it adds, by the use of rhythm, assonance, rhyme and dissonance, a musical parallel to the meaning of the words, so that they are heightened and regain a part of the essence that has been lost to them. When words speak in terms of music, as they do in poetry, they move closer to the reality they seek to form, so that they begin to dance, to move to the measure of their own music. As T. S. Eliot puts it:

> . . . And every phrase
> And sentence that is right (where every word is at home,
> Taking its place to support the others,
> The word neither diffident nor ostentatious,
> An easy commerce of the old and the new,
> The common word exact without vulgarity,
> The formal word precise but not pedantic,
> The complete consort dancing together).

We are inclined to think of dreaming as a means of escape, an interlude in the cycle of our lives, and we speak of returning from our dreams to the world of reality. But, in fact, dreams are an exploration of that reality, an attempt to grasp it; in sleep we open those secret gates to our own deepest nature, and from there we return, refreshed, to ordinary living. It is, of course, for this reason, that all schools of psychology find in their patients' dreams the most exact guide to their inner lives—realities often so painful that we conceal them under seemingly impenetrable disguises; like Kostschei, the magician in Fokine's ballet *The Firebird*, we guard our secrets within a sleep.

The dance is, therefore, a metaphor, expressed in images, of various states of being that are inadequately represented in words. It deals in essences and not in appearances; in the truth, and not in aspects of the truth. As we have seen in considering the *pas de deux*, it is the most human of all the arts, yet at the same time it is a kind of beautiful geometry, continually in quest of perfect form, the search for a perfect line. And these two aspects of the ballet coincide, for as the relationship between the dancers expresses a relationship in nature, the form of the dance structures this on an abstract, universal level. The form of the classical dance is an exact equivalent to the shaping of various stanzas of a poem where rhythm, balance and proportion are essential to contain the emotional or intellectual idea of that poem. Poetry compresses thought, reduces it to the essential words, translates these words into their musical equivalent. In the same manner the dance compresses emotion into a kind of visual shorthand, which we describe as dance-images, while this is clothed in music to give additional substance to the whole.

There is at the centre of all works of art a kind of tension when the relationship between the images is held at its point of most exact balance. One can see this most clearly in painting where the rhythm of a picture depends on the exact relationship between its various parts, both in line and colour, so that to change one would be to destroy the equipoise in which all is held. If, for example, in a painting of Vermeer, a chair could be moved, or the line of a curtain be made to fall at a different angle, altering the perspective and the shadows within it, the painting would disintegrate, lose its essential balance. So in poetry, a line will be destroyed if a rhythm is changed; the musical shape, depending so much upon the play of alternative vowel sounds, can be hopelessly fragmented by a single word improperly placed. Now this is not the conscious achievement of the artist; he creates this sense of structure, music and design by unconscious means, so that he is often unaware, until he has finished his poem, how fastidious has been his choice of words, how exact the dance of syllables within it. An interesting example of this is in Coleridge's "Kubla Kahn", written, he tells us, as a result of a dream, in a kind of trance, interrupted by the arrival of the notorious Person from Porlock who shattered his reverie. Yet the patterning of vowel sounds in this poem is as exact, regular and formal, as if it had been carefully and consciously designed.

One can see from this a close parallel to the art of the classical dance. It is a formal structure, yet it is held at its transitions in the same tension, at the exact point of balance. We are conscious of the dance as it is summarised in a moment of stillness, so that both the movement that preceded it and the movement that will grow out of it are contained together. Both past and present are seen in what Eliot describes as "the intersection of the timeless moment". The dance is absorbed into a pose, however fleeting, and grows out of it; the actual movement and its potential co-exist, harmonise in the line of the dance in the same manner as different harmonies in music will be drawn together in a chord, so that when the music begins again it will be ringed, as it were, with the echoes of notes even then fading into silence.

There are in ballet passages of stillness in a wider sense, held within the swirl of moving dancers, that are among its most sublime images. They have the same effect as a long-held note or trill of the solo instrument within a concerto, heard above the voice of the orchestra, so that one gets the effect of a reflection—the moon or the stooping trees—imprinted motionless upon the surface of moving water. In the dance it is as if the still centre of the music is momentarily made visible, frozen in a pose of immeasurable grace. So in Tudor's *Dark Elegies* a dancer pauses for a moment and draws with her hands a kind of geometrical pattern in the air that is like a desperate cry for a world of order and reason within her atrocious grief. Similarly in the madhouse scene in *The Rake's Progress* one of the ladies on a visit to the asylum stands motionless looking down on the contorted body of the Rake, for a moment lost in her own reveries. Was she a former mistress, one wonders, a friend, or just a woman moved by a curious compassion she did not expect to feel in her empty heart? One of the most beautiful of all these images of stillness within movement is contained in Massine's ballet *Le Beau Danube* when the male dancer stands, arms outstretched in the centre of the stage, while the dancers move around him as the waltz begins. They are like figments of his imagination, caught in the sweep of music that he alone hears, part of his secret world.

In a dream a certain picture will stand out from all that surrounds it, so that this may be all we remember when we wake. So in the classical dance, certain movements seem to summarise all that has gone before, distil into one gesture—like that made by the dancer in *Dark Elegies*—a world of grief or unspoken love. I think particularly of certain moments in the Second Act of *Giselle*—the beginning of the great unsupported *adagio*, her opening solo, her final pose in the exultant music at the end of the ballet—in which an emotion is drawn on the air with a

kind of precision not known in other arts. Here the spirit speaks through the flesh; the heart articulates in a single movement of the arms, in a manner that is more absolute and precise than the lines of any sonnet.

The ballet is in fact the only major art in which the body is also the instrument of that art. The dancer is both the creator and the created; she is her own work of art. She expresses both the vision of the choreographer and her interpretation of that vision, in the same way as a pianist or violinist will give his own view of the music as he understands it. We have, therefore, in the classical dance two related statements: that of the choreographer and that of the dancer, the one expressed as a comment upon the other. No two dancers are alike, even though they dance the same steps; and the eternal fascination of the ballet is in seeing the same portrait through different eyes, each containing a measure of truth, but not the whole truth which is a distillation from an infinite number of separate interpretations.

The great *pas de deux* in Act II of *Swan Lake* can be danced many different ways; the final effect may be tragic, pathetic, grand or simple, yet it is never the whole of the choreographer's vision, which he indeed continues to seek in the performances of many dancers. Like a poet, he may not understand himself the full implication of his work; it remains hidden to him also, and it is for a dancer to seek it out. For the ballerina in a work like *Giselle* we have at once a search and a new creation, so that what she discovers within the role will be part of the inheritance of her successors whose aim will be to re-interpret this for their own generation.

Théophile Gautier, greatest dance critic of the nineteenth century, continually emphasized the necessity for ballet to remain in this world of dreams, and to have no commerce with the realities of everyday. Only then can it remain an art of essences, for the images must reach us, pure and uncluttered. Critics of the classical dance who object because of the distance it makes from modern life do not understand the power of symbols to reach the heart, and the efforts of certain so-called "modern dancers" to deal with contemporary life in their ballets merely produce a poor imitation, less true than the dance in the streets when the barrel-organ is played by a street musician.

In one of his finest poems Louis MacNeice laments that:

> We cannot cage the minute
> Within its nets of gold.

Yet it is just this ability to catch the fleeting moment, even as a synthesis of past and future, that is unique to the art of ballet. It is, in its broadest sense, an image of life, in that it mirrors the transitory, the moments that glide past us, fade even as we seek to grasp them, fall into the abyss of time never to be recalled. The ballet provides us with a succession of images that form, then drift away, leaving not so much as a shadow on the air, no hint of their passing. It is the most ephemeral of all the arts, continually in a state of flux, of transition, creating with an unsurpassed prodigality, even as each image it creates dies the moment it is born.

It would seem, therefore, as if the so-called abstract ballet contains a greater sense of reality than the dance-drama, and that Fokine, in his emphasis on the unity of the ballet as an expression of drama through music, decoration and the dance, was in fact, incorrect. At the time only one critic, André Levinson, recognised the danger, and was a lone voice in protest against the aesthetics of the Diaghilev Ballet. I think he was right. Ballet is not concerned with make-believe, in the telling of stories; the dance is not a means towards an end, as Noverre and Fokine believed, but an end in itself. This does not mean that there is no place for the dance-drama, only that one must realise that the impact of a dance-drama, like that of an "abstract" ballet is due to the images of the dance created, and not due to any real or imagined synthesis of its different parts. Further, the narrative part of such a ballet is of minor importance, for the dance is not a kind of dumb show, like mime or Punch and Judy, to tell a story that can be told better in words. The essence of ballet is in the dance; it cannot be found elsewhere.

This is not to mean that the dancer is to be dehumanised, as in the later ballets of Balanchine. She must be seen within a relationship with the other dancers on the stage, so that the human element in her art is not lost. There is no contradiction in this: as we have seen, an abstract ballet can contain a far greater human warmth than a dance-drama—a sense of the beauty and impermanence of human relations, as in the case of Jerome Robbins' *Dances at a Gathering* or *In the Night*: these are the ballets without a plot, yet they contain the most profound drama in their exploration of a loving relationship, the most poignant truth.

As we construct our dreams from the facts of our own life— our friends, our encounters, even the rooms we live in and the job at which we work—so the ballet takes the movements of ordinary life and transforms them. The vocabulary of the classical dance with its leaps, runs and turns is the visible language of every day, refined and shaped into a work of art. But unlike ordinary movement, which is directed always towards a goal, the steps of a dance are an end in themselves. Further, while so many of our movements are an instinctive reaction to an outside event, indeed we are hardly aware that we make them, in the dance every movement is a willed act, created solely for its own beauty and emotional truth. It is as if we were in control of our dreams.

Like a dream also, the dance is outside time, or rather, it creates its own time scale. For example, the whole adolescence of Princess Aurora is compressed into less than forty minutes of dancing in Act I of *The Sleeping Beauty*, in the same manner as we might review a whole section of our life through successive images in a dream, each of which is an abstract, possibly of years of living. The ballet is this same self-contained world where time is not measured by the striking of the hours, but only by the changing rhythms of the dance, so that it will seem to be lengthened in *adagio* or in a slow *enchaînement* just as it will be compressed during a passage of *allegro* dancing. The Second Act of *Giselle* occupies the span of one night, not by the omission of certain incidents, as would be the case of a play where the author must be selective of his material and precise about the span of time which his play covers, but by compressing a whole series of shifting emotional relationships within a few dances. So also, in John Cranko's *The Taming of the Shrew*, the courtship of Katherine, all its fluctuations of mood from her first rejection of Petruchio to her final acceptance, is shown in a single *pas de deux*.

As the classical dance uses for its material the refinement of ordinary movement, elaborated though it is and much extended, in the same way it presents our emotional life to us in the form of symbols, either in the images of the dance itself or in the character of the figures within a ballet. A world of love is contained in the classical *pas de deux*, where the ballerina's *arabesque* as it unfolds is also a perfect image of the opening of her heart to love. Similarly the poses *en attitude* taken by the ballerina in the *rose adagio* are the most exact symbol of her growing independence and the pride of newly discovered youth. She is free, the pose tells us, and she is free to love, to choose quite simply the one she is to love, or the one whose love she is free to reject. In the transitions during the *adagio* in the Second Act of *Swan Lake*, we are shown, in a series of *arabesques* of different character, the transformations from fear to reassurance to awakening love. Certain steps are in themselves equated with a single emotion, such as the *ballottés* used to denote Giselle's happiness in her opening dance of Act I, or the *grands ietés* of Aurora on her final entry in Act I of *The Sleeping Beauty*. Yet these can be shaded by the use of different stresses in their performance, or by variants to their basic design, in the same manner that our emotions shade one into another and are never presented to us whole. Serge Lifar has said that the dance "exteriorises the song hidden in daily life", but it is a song with many tones to it, many shadows and ambiguities that can be expressed only in movement.

We are able to see how close the ballet is to the world of dreams in the manner its choreographers personify emotional states in terms of character. The image of the Rose in *Le Spectre de la Rose* is a perfect symbol of nostalgia, or the craving for romantic love, where the dream of youth is shattered by awakening to the empty dawn. Odile is the personification of envy and malice, Petroushka of frustration and inarticulate dreams, Una in Ashton's ballet *The Quest*, the spirit of truth and innocence. The greatness of Fokine's *Petroushka* is in its use of dance symbolism, so that his central character is at the mercy both of a heartless love (the Ballerina) and brute sensuality (The Blackamoor) and is powerless to overcome either, yet he recognises that each may well be a part of himself that he disowns. These characters are as much fantastical, as much real in a deeper sense, as are the figures that nightly dance through our dreams.

So, too, the great themes of the classical ballet—of love, of betrayal and reconciliation—are the material both of our conscious and unconscious life. In sharing these experiences with the dancers we are not escaping from reality, but freeing ourselves from the trivia of daily life to the larger freedom of the world of imagination and dreams. For ballet is a portrait of life, drawn more freely and with a wider scope than any other art can offer us. The dance is an abstraction of human life, contained within a whole series of linked images, each of which is an image of the whole, continually reflecting one upon another, so that we are able to see many different aspects of our emotional life from many angles, the totality of which (though it can never be reached) would be to see that truth in its entirety. If we can never achieve that, at least we can find in the dance the hidden language of our dreams.

6. Form and Design

We must now consider the classical dance as a design, set within a framework of music, no longer as a game or a dream, but as an exposition of sublime logic in movement. We are able to observe this more clearly in the classical dance than in any other form of dancing, since the forced "turn-out" of a dancer's physique allows us to see her performance with a kind of openness and clarity unique to the classical style. It is, of course, a distortion of nature, since our feet are not designed to be placed almost at right angles to our body, but paradoxically it creates a natural spaciousness in movement that could have been obtained in no other manner. In the same way, the use of *points* is unnatural, yet without it the dancer would not achieve the speed, lightness and spirituality that is one of the features of the classical dance. It seems that in order to tame nature, one must first abuse it; in that sense only, a ballerina (the highest type of dancer) is an artificial being, created as an instrument to display, with the utmost clarity, a formal art.

The quality of movement she creates is, of course, mainly sculptural. One grows to understand her art by observing it as it is set at various angles to oneself, so that each one places her in a new perspective. This can be achieved in a simple way, as in the *pas de deux* of Petipa, where the ballerina takes up a pose—usually either an *attitude* or an *arabesque*—and is turned slowly by her partner, so that we may study this at many different angles. The pattern grows more complex as she forms new studies in line, these also taking on a different perspective as she is presented to the audience by her partner. An *arabesque* set at right angles to the audience, has a quite different aspect if it is seen at quarter or three-quarter face; similarly an alteration to the placing of the arms will change the whole balance of the composition. A beautiful effect is sometimes obtained when the ballerina grows slowly into a pose: she may, as in a section of the final *pas de deux* in *The Sleeping Beauty*, rise from the ground as her partner draws her upwards, and the pose has something of the effect of a flower opening its petals until it achieves its fullest bloom. Ashton uses the same effect in the final *pas de deux* between Oberon and Titania in *The Dream*, but here in a reverse manner, so that the ballerina's pose begins to disintegrate from its formal design, falling into more broken lines, as that same flower might shed its petals against the wind. In each case these movements have a profound emotional effect, since they denote both acceptance and surrender on the part of the ballerina, and are thus highly appropriate as symbols in a love duet.

From these differing approaches we reach a profound understanding of the ballerina as a formal design, since all her attitudes coalesce in the mind as a single entity, and one is able to grasp their relationship one to another. We have in fact observed a totality of design, seen in the unfolding of different poses, that draws together in our mind to form a whole. This is also true in a ballerina's *variation*, at the end of which she contains all the movements that she has completed, while, at the beginning, she summarises all that she has the potential to achieve. In each case her repose is a meaningful stillness, in no way a dead or final thing.

The classical ballet is also a ritual, a form of expression, both of the human and the Divine, that has its roots deep within the consciousness of mankind. We find it in the liturgy of the church, the ceremonials of state, in the elaborate customs of everyday life such as weddings and funerals. Yet these have their beginning far beyond our civilisation: the tribal dance, the funeral procession, the marches of primitive armies were essentially ritualistic. Men feel themselves, even today, insecure in the world; they need the comfort of familiar rites, just as they need the mysteries that surround them to be explained in ritualistic terms, so that through these symbols, these rites, they may feel at one with their companions. So it is in the classical ballet with its elaborate processions, its court dances: this is a world in which we feel secure, because those who take part in these rituals seem to understand their meaning, and this brings us peace. I think it is important not to minimise this element in the classical ballet; it answers a need in our own times, since we are starved of symbols and live in a world almost entirely materialistic, one that has no place for mystery.

For we are dealing with something greater than a theatrical art: we are dealing with the central mystery of human expression. It is beyond our understanding how certain movements in themselves have the power to summarise an emotional state; it is a thing we recognise in others, for we communicate in sign language as well as words, and it is something we recognise in the ballet, so that there can be no doubt in the meaning the choreographer wishes to convey. It is, of course, far more than sign language. This does exist in the classical ballet in the form of mime which is little more than a dumb show without much artistic or emotional relevance, and it plays a very small part in modern ballet. No, truly expressive movement, though it can be refined, elaborated and codified, as in the classical dance, belongs to our instinctive, unconscious life. We assimilate its language every day: we note, for example, that when a man smiles, we must look also for the clenched fist; we observe the raised eyebrows, the side-long glance, the movement of the hands towards us or against us. We do not reason about such things; we leave that to the psychologists, but we accept them as part of our world, finding ourselves often in trouble if we read the signs incorrectly, so that a young man may get his face slapped rather than enjoy the kiss he was expecting, or we may commit a serious social gaffe if we misjudge the reactions of others. The dance has absorbed all this, and the classical dance has formalised it, but so basic is movement to our emotional life that it is difficult to distinguish form and content in the classical dance, where they are, to a large extent, indivisible.

I think one can best see this connection between form and content within the images of a continuous dance. Not only do they show their relationship to one another in line and balance, but they also have each an individual emotional quality, again interrelated, but distinct. So a single emotion, whether of joy or grief, will have many facets to it, each contributing to our understanding of the whole but each of a different quality. These shifting images blur one into another, retaining a part of themselves in the new phase of the dance as it emerges, giving it additional weight and substance, as a variation in music will always have a common theme, however much it may diverge from it. The ballerina must indicate this continuity in line and emotion by maintaining a long and flowing line, with no breaks or distortions in the dance, but with a series of varied stresses within the musical phrase. A staccato dancer is like a man with a stutter, and she is a distortion of the classical ideal. Yet she can, if she spaces and phrases her dance correctly, produce a kind of harmonious design as intricate as music or architecture.

One must also consider the ballerina being in herself a kind of summary of the movements of the *corps de ballet*. They are her echo, and they give us hints of her dance, but only she is able to present it in its full intricacy and splendour. In the *grand pas* from *Paquita*, Marius Petipa emphasised this by most beautifully arranging the dances of the *corps* to be an exact reflection, almost mirror-like, of the movements of the ballerina. Kenneth MacMillan uses much the same technique in the slow movement of his *Concerto* when three separate *pas de deux* at the back of the stage echo the duet of the principals. The relationship between the ballerina and the *corps de ballet* is not dissimilar to that of the solo instrument in a concerto. She will pick up the themes announced, often very simply and briefly, by the *corps*, elaborate them and return them in a new guise. Sometimes also, as in Ivanov's choreography for *Swan Lake* and in the Second Act of *Giselle*, solo dancers will emerge from the *corps*, dance a few phrases, then return to it again, much in the same manner as, for example, the woodwind section of an orchestra will have its own passages within a symphony.

We feel the movements of the dancers in our own limbs, so that we leap with the ballerina as our hearts have leaped hearing the music that she also hears; we reach forward with her arms; we cover our face with her hands. The dance is the swiftest of all means of communication between human beings: it is the one thing we all have in common, since we can be tone-deaf to music, colour-blind to art, unresponsive to the power of words. But we can all imitate one another in the dance; it is as catching as measles. Whether it is the chanting, stamping congregation at Revivalist meetings, the gyrating of young people at "pop" festivals or the swaying crowds at football matches—all of them are dancing.

There have been, in the long history of the dance, certain great artists who have been able to achieve the closest possible sense of identification with their audience, from the days of Carlotta Grisi to Dame Margot Fonteyn. How this is achieved remains a mystery, but it seems to lie in part in the total sincerity of the ballerina that is, in some way, communicable to the spectators. With them dancing is not make-believe, but the language of their own hearts; their commitment to the role is so absolute that they seem to live it with their own being. Nor is this something recognised only by those familiar with the ballet. Anna Pavlova danced throughout the world, mainly to audiences entirely ignorant of the ballet, yet she produced in them a response so great that her dancing became a personal communion between herself and each member of that audience, with whom she shared all the secrets of her heart. In our own generation Margot Fonteyn has been loved in the same way, both by the sophisticated and also by those with no real understanding of her art.

It is not just a matter of personality, for that is often an outward thing, a projection of self towards the audience that is more likely than not to be vain, egotistical and insincere. It is something more mysterious than that—a sense that one is admitted to or has overheard a private dialogue between the ballerina and the music, and that one can therefore share in the creative process as the artist experiences it. Unlike acting, where a performance once learned can be repeated nightly, even for months, and vary little in detail, classical dancing must be created at every performance, since it relies upon a personal response to the music that can never be automatic, but must be achieved and maintained from second to second. Great dancing can never be imitative, for it springs from the deepest level of the personality, where there can be no tricks, no lies with technique, no sham. It is the working of the conscious will upon the instincts, the shaping of an inner dream.

In the last analysis, however, one is left with the dancer alone on the stage, as she waits for the music to begin. In the great classical ballets of Petipa and also in *Giselle* this moment is perhaps the most exciting and beautiful of all. She stretches out her arms wide to embrace us all, so that together we seem to be waiting for the music to draw her into her secret world, that of pure imagination, where she invites us to join her. She moves, with the music, into her other dimension where, as Eliot puts it, "dream and reality cross" and the world of formal beauty, that is now becoming lost to us in an ugly mechanistic age, is part of the landscape we and the ballerina share. She has, within her limbs, an infinite potential of movement; she is compact of all beautiful lines which, with huge prodigality, she will display before us, letting them fade one into another, or else, holding them in a series of poses, so that we can explore their secret harmonies. Here she shares in the Divine Act, the act of creation—is one with the movements of the clouds, the rivers and the trees, at one with us whose movements she has taken over, shaped and transcended, at one with the whole giant rhythm of creation. It is extraordinary that this art, that can open up for us such immense perspectives, is still in certain quarters dismissed as trivial and academic: is it some exhaustion of the human spirit that makes it considered so?

The dance is ended, and the ballerina in her final pose summarises all that she has been; all the movements that are now completed are at rest with her, seek in her a new beginning. For her there is only the search, within the music, the choreography, within her own heart, for this one, final gesture that will summarise all. It can never, of course, be attained; like the *mot juste*, it is eternally just beyond one's hand, though one may reach out a thousand times to grasp it and reach in vain. She is herself the poet as she is the poem; she is a multitude of unspoken words.

7. The Image

The mysteries of the dance, like those of its sister art poetry, cannot be caged in words, for the dance belongs to space and light and the free air. All one can do is glimpse its meaning, as shadows are seen that move beneath the sun. This much, however, we do know: that each shares the same creative impulse, and develops out of consciousness in an identical way. It is, therefore, helpful to study poetry and the dance, each at the moment of conception, so that one may gain some insight into their essential being. The poets are, not surprisingly, more articulate than the choreographers in this respect, but it is clear that they speak a common language and deal in similar terms.

The initial concept of a poem comes to the poet often at unexpected moments, and always un-announced. It may be first that he is conscious of a sudden intensity of emotion—whether of joy or grief—for which he can find no reason. There is a sense of inner excitement, of heightened awareness, so that people in the street, or the pictures and furniture of his room, take on a new vividness, a kind of sharpness of outline. Then the poetic experience begins, either as a sense of rhythm or design, a single word, a complete or broken image, or a whole sentence, isolated in space but full of hidden meaning. T. S. Eliot has described this in his essay, *On Poetry and Poets*, when he writes: "I know that a poem, or a passage of a poem may tend to realise itself first as a particular rhythm before it reaches expression in words, and that this rhythm may bring to birth the idea or the image."

One sees, at once, the close connection between this idea and the initial vision of the choreographer, sensed in a rhythm that is, itself, productive of an image of the dance, from which the work begins to grow. Jerome Robbins has told us how his masterpiece, *Dances at a Gathering*, began as a single *pas de deux* to Chopin's music, from which it proliferated into a whole series of dances, growing from those initial images. Many choreographers, of whom Ashton is the supreme example, work directly with the dancers whom they may ask to improvise or shape a series of variants on a single pose, one of which he would recognise as the one he required, so that the creative process is continually at work during rehearsals of the ballet. Dame Ninette de Valois, on the other hand, had each movement exactly mapped out in her mind and written down in her own notation, before even the dancers assembled. It is, however, likely that the first idea for the ballet suggested itself to each choreographer in the same terms as the poem came to Eliot—in a rhythm, an isolated image formed in the void. Valéry's description of the poet can here be exactly applied to the choreographer, when he says: "he is the cool scientist, almost an algebraist in the service of a subtle dreamer." Thus the ballet is created—from dreams, from a secret reverie, and is worked out in the formal design of the classical dance that is a kind of sublime geometry, an algebra shaped in the perfect logic of its own being.

The choreographer is, of course, profoundly influenced by the music, whether this has been specially composed for his ballet, in which case he is able to give a guide-line to the composer, or whether it is chosen later, when the concept of the ballet is more fully developed in his mind. It is most likely that the choreographer today will be drawn to an existing score that corresponds to his mental picture of the ballet, or the ballet may find its first images as he listens to a certain piece of music. Here again the experience of the poet is astonishingly similar. Schiller, for example, writes as follows: "The perception with me is at first without a clear and definite object; this forms itself later. *A certain musical mood of mine precedes* and only after this does the poetical idea follow." (My italics.)

I think we can say that the initial concept of a ballet, like a poem, is marked by a sense of music, generating images to which it gives shape and meaning, and that these images proliferate into the design of the whole work. We can see this in Tetley's great ballet, *Voluntaries*, to which I have referred in previous pages. This ballet is a visible exploration of the creative process, following the lines as I have described them: first the initial image; then the image caught up in the music (the great opening chord of the organ); then the flowering of new images from it, taken up and passed from one dancer to another, almost in the form of the development section of classical music. Throughout the ballet reference is made to the first steps of the dance, performed in silence, either by repetition, or by variation on a similar design, and it comes to its close in a repeat of the opening statement. I believe, as I have said earlier, that this ballet has a wider implication, but I think it is an almost perfect example of the working of the creative process as the poets have described it.

A ballet, no more than a poem, is not an isolated creation of the choreographer; it is a summary of his own vision of life, gained over many years, drawing its material both from the inner and outer world. Sir Osbert Sitwell has told us in his autobiography *Left Hand, Right Hand!* how on victory night in 1918 he was with Léonide Massine in the crowds in Trafalgar Square and outside Buckingham Palace, and how the great choreographer watched them dancing together, . . . "so practical an artist," (Osbert Sitwell writes) "and in spite of the weighty traditions of his art, so vital in the manner in which he seizes his material from the life around him, he was watching intently the steps and gestures of the couples, no doubt to see if any gifts to Terpsichore could be wrung from them." It is for this reason that the ballet is so human an art, so rich in its associations, so close to our own living, for it draws its material from the common life of the world. This has been most beautifully and movingly put by Rilke, one of the greatest of all explorers of this strange territory between reality and dreams: "For it is memories that matter", (he says). "Only when they have turned to blood within us, *to glance and gesture,* only then can it happen that in a most rare hour the first word of a poem arises in their midst and goes forth from them." (My italics.) This passage brings to mind the ballets of Antony Tudor, where memory is enclosed within a glance, grief made articulate in the lowering of an arm, the tilt of a head. *Lilac Garden,* that almost Proustian recollection of time past with all its sad gifts of memory, is composed of just such glances, such gestures. It is interesting that during a rehearsal of his ballets Tudor will sometimes halt the dancer and ask her what the gesture she had just made meant to her, for in his ballets there is no movement without meaning, none that does not open for us some dark and hidden region of the heart. His art is the summary of a lifetime, memory that "has turned to blood within us".

Before I leave the question of the initial moment of creation of both a dance and a poem, I should like to add the testimony of Gérard de Nerval, the French imagist poet who had a profound influence on the development of modern poetry both in France and Britain. I have chosen it because it is essentially a visual image of the poem, and thus most closely relates to the apprehension of the choreographer: "I saw", (he writes) "vaguely drifting into form, plastic images of antiquity, which outlined themselves, became definite and seemed to represent symbols of which I only seized the idea with difficulty." It must have been in such a manner that the poses of *L'Après-Midi d'un Faune* first suggested themselves to Nijinsky, as "plastic images of antiquity" which he was to bring into extraordinary form by the force of his creative imagination.

No poet studied in closer detail his own craft than Paul Valéry, and he discussed in great detail the working of his poetic imagination from the moment of creation. It is significant that Valéry considered the dance to be the highest form of artistic expression in that it dealt with poetic essences and in matters beyond verbal analysis; it is, he considered, an art of pure form, unsullied by any of the associations from which he sought to liberate his own poetry. In two books, *L'Ame et La Danse* and *Degas, Danse, Dessin,* he wrote of the dance as an art that is able to translate the ineffable, the essential truth of human emotion. One can see how closely he related the dance with the poetic impulse when he writes of his poem "Le Cimetière Marin" that it sprang "from a rhythmic figure, empty, or filled with meaningless symbols which obsessed me for some time". Elsewhere he writes that "known objects and beings are in a way *musicalised*; they have become *resonant to each other* and as though tuned to our sensibility".

In the same manner the images of the dance are not merely seen by us consecutively, like beads strung on a necklace, but reflect one another and interrelate, become, as Valéry puts it, "resonant to each other". Thus our recollection of each step or of an *enchaînement* is superimposed one on the other in the imagination to form a single whole, a kind of dream architecture, a palace of our own mind. A dance develops organically, being itself shaped like a wider image of its separate parts, creating a unity not only of design but emotion, the same unity, in fact, of a poem that is held together by a series of related images, themselves aspects of a whole that is the truth of the poem.

As well as sound, individual words have their own shape, and the design of a poem, like that of a dance, depends on the combination of the shape, sound and resonance of individual words, linked into a series of related images. I do not wish to go so far as the theorists of eurythmics and state that every word has its visual equivalent, for the poetry of the dance is more complex than this, but unless we understand that the words of a poem have their own shape, we shall gain no appreciation of poetic design, or an equivalent design in the dance. For as movement is a merging of both form and content, poetry is a combination of words and meanings, and both are expressed in imagery. They meet on a common ground, for they speak in metaphor, which is a heightening of literal truth to express ideas that cannot be spoken in prose. In Dryden's magnificent phrase a poet and a choreographer "move the sleeping images of things to the light".

Like a dance, the poem is shaped with the same concern for line and balance. This it achieves apart from its rhythmic basis by changes of pace and differences of texture, brought about by the patterning of vowel sounds, so that a new musical line is set in counterpoint against the basic rhythm. It allows for hidden pauses and varying *tempi* by means of caesura, or by sudden extensions through enjambment or a deliberate use of long vowel sounds to hold back its advance. One can see how close this is to great classical dancing, where the ballerina will form the dance in counterpoint against the music by the use of unequal stresses, changes of speed and emphasis, in the dynamic shaping of each musical phrase. There are few moments in classical dancing more moving than when the ballerina deliberately slows down a phrase and sets it, with a particular emphasis, within the *enchaînement* as a whole. It may be a slow *pirouette* or a turn *en attitude*; suddenly she will make it gleam, glow in its own soft radiance, like a single pearl.

When we read a poem silently to ourselves, we hear its music inwardly as we might were we to read a musical score. In the same manner we hear inwardly the music that, in our imagination, accompanies a silent dance. It is, however, music that gives to the dance the same dimension as we find when we read the poem aloud. A beautiful example of musical texture, created in verse by the use of different vowel sounds, is contained in the following extract from a poem by Edith Sitwell that, in its last line, suddenly slows the pace most exquisitely, as the dancer might by extending in movement a musical phrase. It is a poem and it is also a dance; it is, like a dance, a flowering of connected images within a musical whole.

> Most lovely Shade . . . Syrinx and Dryope
> And that smooth nymph that changed into a tree
> Are dead . . . the shade, that Æthiopia, sees
> Their beauty make more bright its treasuries—
> Their amber blood in porphyry veins still grows
> Deep in the dark secret of the rose
> And the smooth stem of many a weeping tree,
> And in your beauty grows.

It was Walter de la Mare who maintained that poetry should be composed of a pattern of strong and weak lines, so that one did not obtain too great a density of images. I think this is an important point in relation to the dance, where the ballerina must allow the stresses to fall unequally, so that certain passages stand out while others are passed over with the minimum amount of emphasis. A good choreographer will compose in the same manner, so that his images have space around them, and are set between linking movements that carry little emotional weight. The ballets of Frederick Ashton are a perfect example of this, where a dance or an emotional relationship is frozen within a pose, or a *pas de deux* gains a sudden beauty by the juxtaposition of a new or highly original image against poses of a more formal and expected design. Certain poets, for example Hopkins and Dylan Thomas, aim at so great an intensity of effect that there is no sense of space and light within their verse; it has, in my view, too great a density, too monotonous a rhythmic pulse binding the poem together. The same compression is seen in many of the ballets of John Cranko, where the images crowd one upon another, so that the effect is cramped, exhausting to the eye and finally self-defeating. In some way his dances seem to be huddled together, where a great profusion of ideas leave the spectator unable to discover those in which the emotional content of the dance is most clearly expressed.

The dance, like poetry and song, should have a clear, uncluttered line, where the body must be free and allowed to sing with a wide spaciousness of movement. Its images will strike one with more power and greater beauty if they are set within the clarity of simple movement, as the figures in the great paintings of Italian art are set against a landscape that is both distant and serene. A choreographer should not try to over-decorate his line, and should aim for the huge simplicities of the greatest poetry. The dance must be direct, yet full of hidden resonance; it must move one's heart, like poetry, by the magical power of quiet images, as, for example:

> Yet we'll go no more a-roving
> By the light of the moon.

Herbert Read defined the highest form of poetry as "absolute poetry" in which the poem relates most closely to music and is not a means to express any idea outside its own nature. It is completely self-contained, its own world, its own reality. We

cannot paraphrase it, any more than one could give a pictorial
or emotional illustration of the greatest passages in symphonic
music. Yet it will move us profoundly, catching us up into its
secret world. Such a poem, for example, is the exquisite song
from *Measure for Measure*:

> Take, o, take those lips away,
>   That so sweetly were forsworn;
> And those eyes, the break of day,
>   Lights that do mislead the morn!
> But my kisses bring again,
>   Bring again;
> Seals of love, but seal'd in vain,
>   Seal'd in vain!

or, in T. S. Eliot's *The Hollow Men*:

> Eyes I dare not meet in dreams
> In death's dream kingdom
> These do not appear:
> There, the eyes are
> Sunlight on a broken column
> There, is a tree swinging
> And voices are
> In the wind's singing
> More distant and more solemn
> Than a fading star.

This "absolute" poetry relates to the greatest compositions of
the classical ballet, as, for example, the *rose adagio* in *The
Sleeping Beauty* where the dance, with its mysterious associations, exists in its own right and is an end in itself, uncluttered
by the memories of everyday, a statement of formal beauty of
the most intense kind. Prose is a functional art; it exists as a
means towards the transmission of ideas; when these are
grasped the prose ceases to exist. Poetry, however, like the
dance, is an end in itself: to ask what an *arabesque* means is as
foolish as to ask what is the meaning of a rose.

One of the essential features of the poetic image, as with the
image of the dance, is that it reaches directly to the subconscious
where such images are gathered and stored. The music that

accompanies the dance fulfils the same role in achieving this as does the rhythm of the poem; each lull us into tranquillity where, in Yeats' words "the mind, liberated from the pressure of the will, is unfolded in symbols". It is, I suppose, a form of hypnosis in which the critical and analytical functions of the mind are neutralised, leaving ourselves open to receive the symbols of the dance, pure and uncluttered by rationalisation. Poetry and the dance bypass the reason; they reach directly to the heart, to the source of our inner life.

It is, of course, true that poetry and the classical dance are both highly artificial. In a banal sense, one could ask what young man would address his girl friend in regular five-stress lines, any more than he would express his love for her in a series of *pirouettes*. If he did that in ordinary life she would have every right to be concerned. Yet to express emotion rhythmically is fundamental to all human beings, from the war-chants of primitive tribes to the acres of versification written by young men and girls in love. Where there is rhythm, there is the greatest intensity of life, and it is towards that intensity that the poet and choreographer forever strive. This is why poetry and the dance can move us so deeply, for they reach the deepest springs in our consciousness where rhythm finds its own echo. The dance and the dancer are one, and we are one with the dancer also, moving with her limbs, speaking ourselves through all her glances.

A dance interpreted with true understanding will re-create that vision that first presented itself to the choreographer, the pure idea at the beginning of his creation. It may be, and probably is with most dancers, only an approximation to what he first envisaged, but with the greatest of dancers her movement will return to that first source of their being in the secrecy of his mind. For she is the poet's dream, a figure from his reverie, more secret, more beautiful than the dreams of night, more mysterious also; she is the voyager to those most distant lands of the imagination, and only the poet can accompany her there.

8. The Dance and Music

Having studied the dance from various angles, it may now be possible to see the art of ballet more clearly as a whole. Of all arts it is the most elusive, since its total impact depends upon the fusion of several disparate elements into a unity that may only be achieved for a brief, fleeting instant during the performance. Yet even as you seek to grasp it, the moment has gone and is no more than a recollection, a memory of certain steps framed within a phrase of music, now as evanescent as that music when it is no longer heard. But it is at these moments that the great reconciliations of art are made, when the dance catches fire, blazes in its own light.

The dance is elemental: it belongs to the elements of earth and air, of fire and water; it is a part of nature, where the spirit has made the body its means of expression, and seeks for that unity underlying all created things. The dancer will float, like the vision of a cloud, or the moving of the autumn mist; she will blaze with all the brilliance of the sun at noon, or the fire that burns at the heart of a diamond. Her arms will ripple like the moving waters; her limbs shimmer like a distant sea. Yet she is also a creature of earth, warm, sensual and free, and she has a kinship with all that lives from the plants, the shifting leaves to the animals and birds. As she can in her dance imitate these things, she can make us part of them and let us see how all nature moves to the same rhythm, the same dance. As André Levinson puts it:

Here the fusion of organic nature with abstract form is miraculously achieved. The dancer opens like a flower; she is no longer even a woman; being more like nature than a human being, she breathes like a plant exhaling perfume. Then, once the movement has been executed, she becomes an abstract symbol created by intelligence. Or else she leaps up and flies off like a dragon-fly, a butterfly or a swan—all symbols of radiant and winged creatures— to become, once her *enchaînement* is complete, a statue, the epitome of balance held for eternity, the incarnation of immutable beauty. The dancer, constantly oscillating between profound instinct and design in space, achieves what our friend André Lhote once called "the translation into plastic terms of the *coup de foudre*".[1]

This elemental aspect of the dance is quaintly and rather beautifully described in a poem by George Herbert, a poet who was at once a mystic yet also a man of common sense and a rough earthy wisdom.

> Man is all symmetry,
> Full of proportions, one limb to another,
> And all to all the world beside:
> Each part may call the furthest brother
> For head and foot have private amity,
> And both with moon and tides.

It is the essential function of the poetic image that it is able to give us some insight into the relationship of all things, to set them in contrast to one another, so that we are able to see, if only dimly, how they are all part of the whole. It is all a dance, we say in a moment's vision: it is all one.

In the ballet, the dancer is at one with the music, and she also exists in a relationship, both spatial and musical, to her companions on the stage. She is at one with the choreographer's vision, at one with the designer's world. You cannot, without distorting that reality, separate its individual parts, since they all refract light, each contributing to the whole. The images they form together are continually being displaced by others; like a kaleidoscope, the pattern is reformed, giving us a new insight, a different perspective.

[1] For French text, see page 173.

If one takes the primary elements in this pattern, those of the choreography and the music, one cannot detach these from the dancer herself; not only does she weld them together, but she also adds to them her own vision of their nature. This vision of the music cannot be identical to that of the choreographer, since no two human beings look upon the same thing from the same angle. It is a complementary vision, but not an identical one. Similarly the choreography is not one man's interpretation of the music, so much as an attempt to find a visual parallel to the composer's inspiration.

It is probably true that when the composer works in collaboration with the choreographer, as in the ballets of Petipa, it is likely that there will be a closer accord between the two visions, but on the whole the composer is likely to suffer, for he cannot give his best work when his wings are clipped in such a manner. Apart from that of Tchaikovsky, very little ballet music, written at the direction of the choreographer, is of the highest class; in the main, it is journeyman stuff, like that of Minkus, and provides little more than a rhythmic basis for the dance. There are, of course, exceptions; for example Gavin Gordon's music for Ninette de Valois' great ballet, *The Rake's Progress*, is highly dramatic, full of detailed descriptions of the drama from the absurd trillings of the ballad singer in the orgy scene to the last shuddering gasps of the Rake in the madhouse. As the inspiration for the ballet came from Hogarth's paintings, so the music also is a painting in sound; it is highly visual, and so provides an almost exact musical parallel to Hogarth's designs; at the same time it is shallow emotionally, and provides little more than surface effects of great brilliance in the same way as does Rex Whistler's beautiful drop-curtain. It is music descriptive of action, but it does not illuminate the action with any insights of its own.

During the eighteenth and nineteenth centuries it was taken for granted that the choreographer would dictate to the composer the type of music he required even to the most exact details of phrasing, atmosphere and metre. We have, for example, the most precise instructions given by Petipa to Tchaikovsky for the opening scene of *Casse-Noisette*, in which the composer was entirely subservient to the choreographer, even a composer as eminent and vastly gifted as Tchaikovsky. Petipa instructed him in this manner:

No. 1. Musique douce, 64 mesures.
No. 2. L'arbre s'éclaire. Musique pétillante de 8 m.
No. 3. L'entrée des enfants. Musique bruyante et joyeuse de 24 m.
No. 4. Le moment d'étonnement et d'admiration. Un tremolo de quelques mesures.
No. 5. Marche de 64 mesures.
No. 6. Entrée des Incroyables. 16 m. rococo (tempo menuet).
No. 7. Galop.
No. 8. L'entrée de Drosselmeyer. Musique un peu effrayante et en même temps comique. Un mouvement large de 16 à 24 m. La musique change peu à peu de caractère, 24 m. Elle devient moins triste, plus claire et enfin passe à la gaîté . . . Musique assez grave de 8 et temps d'arrêt. La reprise des mêmes 8 m. et aussi temps d'arrêt. 4 mesures avec des accords d'étonnement.
No. 9. 8 m. d'un temps de mazourka, 8 autres m. de mazourka. Encore 16 m. de mazourka.
No. 10. Une valse piquée, saccadée et bien rhythmée. 48 m.

On comparison with the final score, one can see that, on the whole, Tchaikovsky kept close to Petipa's instructions, although there are variants, no doubt as a result of further consultation as the creation of the ballet progressed. After the commencement of rehearsals Petipa fell ill, and his assistant, Ivanov, then took over, so that it may well be—as he was not so autocratic a figure as Petipa—that Tchaikovsky allowed himself some further amendments to the score, with which he was not (quite rightly) satisfied.

We can see, however, that Petipa was merely following the precedent established by choreographers of the previous century, including Noverre and Bournonville, its two most celebrated exponents. In the preface to his *Lettres sur la Danse et les Ballets*, published in 1760, Noverre writes:

My poem once conceived, I studied all the gestures, movements and expressions which could render the passions and sentiments arising from my theme. Only after concluding this labour did I

65

a

summon music to my aid. Having explained to the composer the different details of the picture which I had just sketched out, I then asked him for music adapted to each situation and to each feeling. In place of writing steps to written airs, as couplets are set to known melodies, I composed, if I may so express myself, the dialogue of my ballet, and then I had music written to fit each phrase and each thought.

Again, as in the case of Petipa, he was not dealing with some hack composer, who would willingly fall in with his ideas; it was to composers of the eminence of Gluck, creator of the music to Noverre's famous ballet *Iphigénie en Tauride*, that such instructions were addressed.

It is interesting that in the next century Bournonville worked to the same principles, though he extends them by subsequently altering his choreography in the light of the music as it had originally been composed to his instructions. We are therefore at the mid-point in the history of the relationship between choreographer and composer, as it was taken up by Fokine and Stravinski in *The Firebird*, *Petroushka* and *The Rite of Spring*, where they worked as collaborators with equal rights and interests in the ballet. Bournonville, however, writes in very similar terms to Noverre:

> Once the *scenario* has been worked out, I shut it up in a drawer; after a while I take it out, re-read it, and, if it interests me, if each of its pictures spring to life in my mind, it is ripe for production. Then it is that I apply to a musician. I give him the programme of each scene capable of constituting "a number", after which we discuss its appropriate character and its rhythm. In general, I explain to him, by means of miming, a plan, a sketch of what I wish to do; sometimes I improvise a melody and if it suggests a possible theme the musician notes it immediately and gives it form and modulation.

At the furthest extreme from this is found the attitude of George Balanchine who maintains that "I can always invent movement and sometimes it can be fitted into the right place, but this is not choreography. The music dictates the whole shape of the work". And not only the shape, one might add, but also every detail, so that at times in Balanchine ballets the dancers appear to be doing no more than mark time to the music. As a Soviet critic well described it: the dancers dance the notes but not the music. Balanchine has maintained that there is no emotional content in music, and this is seen in his work, where the dancers appear two-dimensional figures, unrelated to one another in the cold spaces where they move.

It is true that in certain ballets like *Serenade, Night Shadow* and *Liebeslieder Walzer* he can create beautiful and emotionally rich movement when he is working to a score that denies his precepts; for one can no more exclude emotion from Tchaikovsky's *Serenade for Strings* than one can from the heart-felt romance of Brahms' waltzes. It seems to me that, if one gives music such predominance, it can only be at the expense of the dancers, and it is not perhaps surprising that the finest and most individualistic dancers produced by the New York City Ballet— Maria Tallchief, Susanne Farrell and Mimi Paul—left the company at the height of their fame. This was particularly sad in the case of Mimi Paul who promised to become one of the few really great dancers of our time.

There is, indeed, a considerable monotony in Balanchine's work, where the range of movement is not equal to the demands the composer makes on it; sometimes the repetition is such that one feels the choreography is interchangeable between ballets. It is a choreography invented, rather than created, and its lack of true musicality, as against musical exactitude, is what, in the last analysis, condemns it to sterility and a dead end in the classical dance.

The ideas of Serge Lifar concerning music and the dance are in direct opposition to those of Balanchine, and, though they have continually been misrepresented to prove that Lifar denies any real place to music in ballet, they are an important addition to the dance aesthetics of our time. Lifar maintains that the dance, by its own essential rhythm, is self-sufficient; the music is able to enrich movement, but it must be as an expression of the essentially rhythmic base of the dance. Lifar argues, very convincingly, that the dance historically preceded music, and that the earliest form of music was that made by the dancer himself to accompany and emphasise his dance. In his important book, *Ballet: Traditional to Modern*, Lifar writes of the subservience of the dance to the music as follows:

> In freely accepting a despotic bondage, ballet has moved counter to its own essence, to itself; it is hindered in its own creation.

Lifar makes an important point, highly relevant to the ballets of George Balanchine, when he writes:

> When I am discussing dancing executed to music I am evidently far from thinking of an interpretation of musical notes by the legs of the *danseur* or *danseuse*. Such a purely mechanical equivalent between music and dancing does not exist, and happily cannot exist, for art vanishes when mechanical dancing begins.

The reconciliation between music and the dance would seem best achieved when composer and choreographer work together to encompass a single vision. The difficulty to this in our time is twofold: first, that few composers are willing to work within the limitations of the dance as seen by the choreographer; secondly, that little modern music has sufficient clarity of line and rhythmic vitality to be suitable for the dance. The greatest modern composer, Benjamin Britten, composed only one full-length ballet score, *The Prince of the Pagódas*, but this was not successful, partly because of the foolish narrative to which he was obliged to write, and also to the weak and derivative choreography of John Cranko, so that the ballet fell into a welcome oblivion. Shostakovitch has never written directly for the ballet, though much of his music, as MacMillan shows in his superb ballet *Concerto*, is highly suitable for the dance; and of twentieth-century composers, apart from Stravinski, whose later music seems to me empty, sterile and basically trivial, only Prokofiev in *Romeo and Juliet* has created a truly danceable score. The modern choreographer, for these and for obvious financial reasons, is thus for the most part obliged to use existing music where the relationship between music and dance is not, in general, as close as it might be if he had worked to a commissioned score.

As an ideal we have the collaboration of Stravinski and Fokine in *The Firebird* and *Petroushka*. In this case they worked independently of one another to express a common vision, and remained equal partners in the venture. However, once again I feel that Stravinski's music is essentially pictorial. It is a higher class than that of Gavin Gordon, but it is, in the main, shallow and composed of brilliant surfaces. His music for *The Rite of Spring* is different in quality, for it seems to come from a much deeper level of his own nature; it is more the anguished cry of one man's tormented spirit that has become universalised in the choreography, rather in the same manner as *The Waste Land* has appeared to be a portrait of a disintegrating civilisation, but was composed as the expression of a personal grief.

Perhaps the two most successful scores ever written for a ballet are Adam's music for *Giselle* and Delibes' music for *Coppélia*. It is, however, likely that they would not survive long in the concert hall, but they provide a series of images very closely related to the choreography, not only in terms of description, but also of emotion. Delibes' score has a kind of bright, paint-box colouring of brilliant, almost child-like simplicity, yet it has also a lyrical heart of great tenderness that is discovered at once in its exquisite opening waltz for Swanhilda's *variation*. While it has its purely descriptive passages, as, for example, the bubbling little tune when Dr Coppélius pours out the wine for Franz in the Second Act, it also contains moments of a kind of shimmering beauty, some of which are quite wasted in the traditional choreography (for example, at the moment when Dr Coppélius wheels Swanhilda on to the stage in the conviction that this is his beloved doll) yet are full of a sense of magic and mystery. Delibes never achieved such an exquisite score again, and his music for *Sylvia* is sadly full of tunes more suitable for a teashop string trio, and dancers have complained that it is almost impossible to take it seriously. It is true, I think, that the composer is profoundly influenced by the libretto, and Delibes could not take the foolish narrative of *Sylvia* seriously any more than Tchaikovsky could that of *Casse-Noisette*, so that both composers here produced work very much below their best standard.

Adolphe Adam's score for *Giselle* is probably the finest piece of music ever composed for a ballet. It may not, by absolute standards, be great music when isolated from the action, but in the theatre it is an equal partner to some of the greatest choreography ever invented. Not only is it masterly in descriptive passages, not just in terms of indicating the action but in seeking out its emotional undercurrent, it is also exquisitely shaped around the choreographic line (especially in the Second Act) where it seems to superimpose an additional visual image over that created by the ballerina, so that it is almost as if another dimension had been added to the dance. In its use of *leit-motivs*, described also in the choreography, it binds the whole work together in a manner that is full of tragic irony, of hidden echoes of extraordinary resonance.

In general, it would seem best to follow the principles of Lifar rather than those of Balanchine: to create the dance to its own rhythms, and then relate these to music in a free, impressionistic association, rather than equating movement to the exact value of each note. There should be a flexible relationship, a constant interchange, so that the choreography is like the solo instrument in a concerto, related to the orchestral accompaniment in the same way, either formally or emotionally. Thus at moments the dance and the music become one; at others they exist in parallel. The dance must, in fact, be the visual equivalent of the vocal line in a song, with the same freedom, the same desire to unite at moments of great emotion. And the dancer is the singer of that song, her phrasing of the musical line the true test of her ability.

Much of the beauty of the greatest choreography is due to such an interchange, where the shifting balance between the two elements at certain moments coalesces into an harmonious image. Antony Tudor, perhaps of all choreographers the most subtle and adventurous in the handling of music, provides many such moments in his greatest ballets; one remembers, in particular, how Caroline, in *Lilac Garden*, turns a sudden, anguished *pirouette* at the side of the stage and her lover emerges from the bushes to hold her on a trill of the solo violin; or how, in *Dark Elegies*, the soloist falls suddenly under the weight of the music, as if her grief were too huge a burden to bear. Michel Fokine's ballets carry the same imprint of great musicality, particularly in *Les Sylphides* where the *lift* to which the ballerina and her partner enter in the final waltz exactly matches the curve of the melodic line; or, in *Carnaval*, when Harlequin and Columbine enter, he dancing to the quavers and she to the semi-quavers of the octave in which the music is contained. An unimaginative choreographer will be deaf to such subtleties; for him the rhythmic beat must be followed at all costs, even to that of boring his audience. For those earnest missionaries of the "Free Dance" who maintain that music can be fully expressed in movement, Lifar has a charming reply: stop your ears, he tells them, and then let me know to what music the dancer performs. It is a short ending to a very long argument.

Dancing to song has been, on the whole, extremely effective in certain ballets, notably in Andrée Howard's exquisite *La Fête Etrange* where the dances to Fauré's songs have a delicacy and fragility that invoke the music with an almost piercing beauty, even to the final moment when the dancers intertwine their hands like the calices of flowers, cupped to hold the music as if it were falling dew. Here indeed the dance is like a still life painting, frozen in a moment of exquisite repose. In Kenneth MacMillan's *Song of the Earth*, beautiful though it is at certain moments, the songs are so deeply emotional they swamp the dancers, for the ballet is not held together in a dramatic way as was Tudor's *Dark Elegies* where dance and music were united in the expression of a common theme.

In ballets composed both for the Nederlands Dans Theater and the Ballet Rambert, much use has been made of electronic music. This provides no more than a kind of tonal background to the dancing that is then formed, as Lifar would admire, solely out of its own rhythms. Here, however, it seems to me that there is too great a divide between music and dancing, while, at the same time, electronic scores are, by their nature, inhuman, cold and often extremely ugly to listen to. They also demand from the choreographer a far higher standard of inventiveness than is usually obtained, since he is without the illusion music can create, where a simple image, exactly shaped to the musical line, will carry far greater force than it would if danced to a basically unemotional score. The choreographer, particularly if he is not experienced, will be driven into endless repetitions, as, for example, in Christopher Bruce's ballet, *Unfamiliar Playground*, created for the touring section of the Royal Ballet in October, 1974. Here his attempt to achieve fugal dance, by one performer imitating a second later the identical movement of another, became very monotonous once one had grasped the style. One had only to compare it in memory with the intricacy in the treatment of a musical fugue that was achieved by Tudor in *The Descent of Hebe*, to realise the need for orchestral or at least piano music in creating complexity of design within a ballet.

The visual relationship between the dance and music is a highly complex one. The music provides the dancer with a kind of invisible support for her limbs, in the same way as it carries her along in the dance. It maintains her in flight, and gives her wings so that she is able to trace those patterns of arcs and circles in the air which are the basis of all beautiful form. The choreographer will therefore be aware both of the rhythmic base of the music and also its linear shape. It is like a sketch on a canvas that the dancer will transform into living colour. He will also take from it what emotional colouring he needs, and here, of course, he deals in a parallel relationship rather than a direct transcription. Most music, whether used for the ballet or not, provides us with a whole spectrum of emotion: we experience not only the emotions of the composer, but we also give to it part of our own emotional life which it re-translates and returns to us. We can never say a piece of music *means* one thing or another in terms of emotion; all that matters, fundamentally, is what it means to us alone. In the ballet, the piano music of Chopin has been used both by Fokine in *Les Sylphides* and by Jerome Robbins in *Dances at a Gathering* and *In the Night*. No three works could be more different in feeling, yet at the same time they are each in total accord with the music. There are, of course, limits to the number of different ways a choreographer can interpret the music, since every piece of music has emotional limits and he could not go beyond these without a sense of disharmony. To make an exaggerated example: one could not set the dances of *Les Sylphides* to the music of *The Rite of*

Spring; the result would be totally ridiculous. It is true that in the Cocteau/Petit ballet *Le Jeune Homme et la Mort*, choreography of great sordidness and brutality was set against music by Bach of an almost celestial tranquillity: but this was a deliberate distortion, made in order to heighten the effect when, at the close of the ballet, music and movement are at last in accord.

There may, of course, be a congruity between the ideas of the choreographer and those of the composer whose music he uses. This is clearly seen in Tudor's *Dark Elegies*, composed to Mahler's *Kindertotenlieder*. The world of the ballet is a barren sea coast (in Nadia Benois' designs rather like the coast of Western Ireland) where the fisherfolk mourn for their lost children. This tragic theme is emotionally close to that of the music which is a series of songs on the same theme. On the other hand, there seems no basis for Tudor's choice of Schoenberg's *Verklarte Nacht* for his ballet *Pillar of Fire*; yet each work deals with violently suppressed passion at a level of great emotional tension, and thus they complement one another. Tudor has always been brilliantly original in his choice of music, sensing at once its hidden emotional core—the morbidity of Chausson's *Poème* for *Lilac Garden*, so self-pitying, so full of shuddering distaste in a world of corrupt beauty; the sour, epigrammatic wit of Richard Strauss's music for his ballet *Knight Errant*; the caustic mockery and fierce social criticism of Weill's music for *Judgement of Paris*, or the full-blown but rather tawdry brilliance of Prokofiev's score for *Gala Performance*. Yet one cannot say that these are the only possible interpretations of the music: there is no finality in a choreographer's statement, but only a matter of visual approximations that emphasize one particular element in a score from a multitude of different emotions contained within it.

So also several choreographers may use the same score for entirely different interpretations. Prokofiev's *Romeo and Juliet* has had many choreographers to present it from various angles; these include Lavrosky, Ashton, MacMillan and Cranko, and it would be impossible to state which version is most true to the music, any more than one could choose between van Manen's and Ashton's interpretation of Ravel's *Daphnis and Cloé*, or the separate versions of *The Rite of Spring* by Nijinsky, Massine, MacMillan or Taras. There are no absolutes in the world of ballet music.

All considerations of music in the ballet lead one back to the dancer, for she is the link between the choreographer and the music; in her movements they find their synthesis, this fusion of perfect grace and architectural design. For the ballerina music is the texture of her dream. It translates what might be otherwise solely physical or mechanical into the singing lines of verse, so that each phrase of the dance is like a section of a poem, set and enclosed in its own music, a bright ring around her. As the music gives emotional colouring to the dance, the ballerina, in fair exchange, explores the music as a visible structure. It is music that gives the classical dance this sense of an endless flow of movement, like the rippling inland of the waves. Indeed if one could imagine the choreographer's vision and that of the composer meeting as two lines in space, at that point of inter-section would be the ballerina, drawing from each its own particular radiance.

The music gives structure to her dance, allowing it to shape itself around the musical line, so that we are able to observe the ballerina as if she created music by the movement of her limbs. Between her and the music there is a constant exchange, in much the same manner as that between the soloist and the orchestra in a concerto. The music not only gives the rhythmic base to her dancing, but also allows the ballerina to make visible its design on the air. She is able, as it were, to draw it in space, tracing the outline of each curve, each leap or fall in the music. At the same time the music gives the dance much of its emotional colouring. The dance absorbs this and then exposes the shape and architectural design of the music. There is a continual reciprocity: the music adds colour to the dance, and this transforms it into movement, giving in return to the music a kind of visual identity it did not have before. The music pro-vides, as it were, the theme; this the ballerina will elaborate and develop, so that when the next section of the music is heard, it has already been given a visual shape which it, in turn, takes up and elaborates.

The absolute test of a great ballerina is in the manner she phrases the music as she hears it. For each dancer this is a personal insight; it is for her to choose what element in the music she will stress, which she will let pass her by; the shaping of each phrase is her responsibility, as if the music were a kind of raw material—for example, the block of stone from which the sculptor is to create his model—and it is for her to form it in accordance with its nature. The shaping of each dance is hidden within the music, as the statue is buried within the stone, and the ballerina must seek for it with all the delicacy and sensitivity of her imagination. It is not something given in the choreography, so that she would only have to imitate what she had been taught, but it is a personal insight into the heart of the music where her dance resides.

Every dancer differs in her attitude to music: some will let their dancing grow almost organically out of it; others will spin it round them like a silken web. They will ride above it, or sink beneath it, as if it were the surface of moving water. At certain moments the greatest dancers give themselves so totally to the music that they move as if in a trance, carried across the stage like Shelley's autumn leaves, "like ghosts from an enchanter fleeing".

Any consideration of music in the ballet must lead one to the thorny question of musicality in dancers. This has long been a source of endless argument, and in their time both Anna Pavlova and Olga Spessivtzeva were accused of being unmusical. The criticism does not come from audiences or critics who, one feels, are looking for something different from the exact marking of the rhythmic beat. For them, the musicality of a dancer is seen in the way she shapes the musical line and phrases the music in her own, original way, combining both of these skills within a unified whole. Lifar again summarises the argument when he writes:

Certain *danseurs* and *danseuses* of genius, such as Anna Pavlova or Olga Spessivtzeva, have occasionally given proof of "a lack of musicality" and lost contact with the music in the midst of a dancing episode, and that has not prevented them from always beginning and ending with the music. At the same time, they gave evidence of an extraordinary musicality, yet that musicality was not, so to speak, musical but dancing. I will go further: I will say that there is never an exact relationship between danced movement and music, *and that there cannot be*. If a spectator believes he observes that coincidence, it is simply that he is the victim of one of those manifold illusions of our art . . . I insist on this fact, that there cannot be exact superposition between these two essential elements of ballet, because a dance step is always instantaneous and shorter in time than that taken by a note of music (one of the most conclusive examples is the jump—the dancer always alights a little in advance of the music). The conductor of the orchestra can, at will, slow down the *tempo*, but we cannot slow down our dancing and mark, for instance, a prolonged pause in the air, or effect a retarded descent.

The argument, I agree, is extended too far, but I have included it in full if only to make the point that there is more to musicality than counting the beats. In general, however, I think it is true that Russian dancers take greater liberties with the music than those of the West: Anna Pavlova was often criticised by her conductor over this, but she stated, quite firmly, that the music was her servant and must play at her bidding, which seems to me an entirely reasonable point of view, though it may make the musical purists shudder—which, in ballet, is no bad thing!

Of course choreographers do vary in their response to the music, and a certain amount of the exploration has already been done for the ballerina, but only in the sense that a map is drawn of a new landscape; it is for her to make the trees grow, the rivers move, the mountains to gather around her: she has to give life and dimension to the chart of this unknown land and make it her own. She has her raw material—the steps of the dance as she has learned it, the shape of the music as she hears it—and it is from these that she must create a new, essential world, made up by the synthesis of these two elements. There must be in her dancing a sense of inevitability; one must feel that there is no other way in which this music could have been shaped, that this is its inner meaning, its central truth.

The audience will be aware of this new element which the ballerina has created by the fusion of music and movement, for they will see the music has been made visible, painted on the air as if by the fine brush-strokes of her limbs. She will, in the truest sense, have made music with her dancing. We must remember also that the visual line has within it a musical element: one speaks of a ballerina whose movement sings, and this is no hyperbole, but is, in fact, an exact description of how she will transform a visual into an aural experience; the long lines made by a ballerina in *arabesque* create exactly the same effect as a long, sweeping tune in music. In the ballet she has to correlate the music of her movements with the visual line in the music, so that both elements are apprehended at the same time in a single audio/visual experience. When we watch the ballet, we are probably not conscious of this, even though we can understand that the relationship between music and dance is much closer than that of mere accompaniment. Each expresses a single vision in their own way, but they are not mutually exclusive of one another, sharing a common language that is heard and seen.

Lifar sees music as a potential master who will sell him into slavery, the kind of servitude the dancers in many works by Balanchine might indeed feel, but this is an exaggeration carried to extreme lengths. The relationship between music and the dance exists in a kind of tension, but this is central to all works of art: the creator must be circumscribed if he is to be free; in the imprisonment of metre and rhyme, for example, the poet will be able to achieve the intensity of the expression that is the purpose of his art.

Certain choreographers have discarded music completely from time to time, and the most successful ballet of this nature in my experience was David Lichine's *La Création*, composed for Roland Petit's company. It was a work of strange beauty, having within it a sense of menace, like the silent conflict between wills, that was both disturbing and haunting; like ghosts, the dancers moved in their strange rite, apart from the audience, remote even from one another, in a kind of emotional void, a rapt self-absorption. Something of the same effect is achieved in Christopher Bruce's ballet, *Unfamiliar Playground*, danced in this case to an electronic score. It is a ballet for five men and five girls, yet there is no sense of any emotional interplay, only a cold, sterile, loveless world, emphasised by the hint of a metal cage that enclosed them. In the first two episodes of the ballet, the men dance alone, then to be followed by the girls; it is only after this that the first approach is made to one another, then quite without feeling or any trace of eroticism. It is as if the dances were set in some bleak, lunar landscape, enclosed in its own solitude, in a strange ice-age of unloved hearts. I have referred previously to the silence in which Glen Tetley's great ballet, *Voluntaries*, begins; here is invoked the brooding dark when silence lay over the earth in that limitless time before the beginning of all things. Used imaginatively in this way, the choreographer may achieve wonderful effects without music, but one could never see it as more than an occasional dramatic device in very particular circumstances.

If a dancer performs without any music, she will create her own music; very distant it will be, heard only by the inner ear, but it will be an unheard music to which she dances. An exact, reverse effect is obtained during the overture to a ballet. Here the music dances; we see it with an inner eye, so that when the curtain rises there is only a sense of continuity; it is not as if the dancing began from that moment, for in the music there has already been this dance. The more musical a choreographer is, the more exact will this transition become. In the ballets of Léonide Massine, for example, like *Gaîté Parisienne*, *Mam'zelle Angot* or *La Boutique Fantasque*, the mocking, ebullient dancers are already present in the overture; when the curtain rises, we see them more clearly, but it is the same dancers that we see, the same world of grotesque movement that they inhabit, so airy, bright and full of mischief.

Music adds colour to the images of the dance in much the same manner as the pattern of vowel sounds adds another dimension to poetry. But this is not something that is imposed upon the dance; rather it grows out of the dancing, so that there is no sense of a clash between the two elements, unless this is deliberately sought for dramatic effect by the choreographer.

The effect must always be one of parallelism, but the two lines —of the music and the dance—draw at moments closer together, even to the extent that for a period they form a single image.

Some of the greatest choreographers have, however, treated music very freely, and have composed dances where the music and the dance exist in counterpoint to one another, only coming together at certain moments, usually either in a *lift* or a pose. Here the music and the dance exist in two separate worlds, and relate by analogy rather than syncopation. The ballets of Jerome Robbins are examples of this. He does not so much shape the musical line or follow its rhythm, but instead treats the music as a kind of back-cloth on which the dancers paint their own designs, so that some of the dances look like free cadenzas round a visual and musical theme. But here again, at moments of the most intense feeling, he will draw the two elements so closely together that they are indistinguishable. His greatest work, *Dances at a Gathering*, is a perfect example of this sort of parallelism; it is almost like a duet between dancers and pianist, where the body sings above the accompaniment of the piano. At the other extreme, Andrée Howard worked so close to the music in her ballets that she seemed to sketch it with an almost Japanese kind of fidelity, so that the dancers' limbs were, in Valéry's beautiful phrase, "like the branches of trees that move in the winds of music". In the very first movement of the opening dance for the Bride in *La Fête Etrange* (her greatest work) the music is drawn with such fine precision that it is entirely reproduced in a single pose. Similarly, in the dances she composed to Fauré's songs in the same ballet, the dancers are made to imitate the vocal line with their arms and torso, while the feet, like a piano accompaniment, form the musical bass.

There must be an immediate communion between audience and dancer, and the music acts as a kind of intermediary between them, the link between their two worlds. The emotional quality of the dances is assimilated intuitively, so that they strike one with a far greater immediacy than is obtainable in any other art, except that of poetry where the assimilation of musical images in the verse is the same as that for the dance.

The quality of the *décor* and costumes is of subsidiary importance, and, indeed, many ballets make a greater impact when danced in practice costume against a plain background. However, it is essential that they share a common mood with the music and the choreography, even to the extent of matching their tonal colour and line, as is the case in Sophie Fedorovitch's designs for Ashton's *Symphonic Variations*.

I think that choreographers must be wary of too close an identification between the music and the dance, when the dance is made to take a subservient role. The ballet is then liable to become dry and academic, if every repeat in the music is represented on the stage by a repetition of movement, while counterpoint is exactly matched by two groups of the *corps de ballet* dancing to the different lines of the music. There is, of course, a place for counterpoint in the dance, as Massine and Fokine have demonstrated in their ballets, but it must spring naturally, either from the nature of the plot—in *Mam'zelle Angot* her dance with the Caricaturist is set exquisitely in counterpoint with the mourning of the Barber and his friends— or its emotional tone, as Tudor in *Echoing of Trumpets* sets the brutish dances of the soldiers against that of the classically orientated movements of the women. But ballets that aim to be visual approximations to the music are seldom effective, if there is no emotional content. Massine's symphonic ballets such as *Choreartium* and *Les Présages* achieved a powerful effect, not by musical parallelism (though of course that was present) but by the highly emotional quality of the score and its dramatic content. In the same way, Balanchine's *Serenade* is a profoundly moving work because of the strange and often poignant relationship between the dancers one to another, even though this cannot be described in literal terms but only in terms of poetic allusion.

A curiosity remains in the use of words as a form of music, only once really successfully achieved in Ashton's *A Wedding Bouquet*. This is, in effect, a concerto for voice and orchestra, in which the music and the dancers echo the verbal rhythm; for example, the phrase "Violet, oh will you ask him to marry you?" in Gertrude Stein's gorgeous pot-pourri of nonsense, becomes a theme on the solo instrument (the voice) which the orchestra and the dancers embellish. The voice even has its own cadenza— an absurd, inconsequential and totally confusing story told to the Bride and the Bridegroom to which they listen with rapt incomprehension. This ballet clearly stemmed from Edith Sitwell's *Façade* to Walton's music, first performed in 1923 and often repeated. *A Wedding Bouquet* must, however, remain an isolated masterpiece, for such a combination of talent is unlikely to be found again.

However, it is the ballerina who, in the last analysis, is the arbiter in this age-long argument between music and the dance when, in each succeeding century, they have fought one another for dominance. For she holds the key; she has to perform the steps and place them in relation to the music, where her taste and musicality are the deciding factors. A great dancer must be profoundly musical; if she is not, she is little better than an acrobat with a limited repertoire of tricks. It is through her judgment that the music is phrased, stressed or lingered over. The choreography is not her creation, but the dance is hers, even to a greater extent than the words of a song belong to the singer, for without her the ballet cannot exist. The music breathes around her, and her body is like the strings of a lyre that it plucks magically in passing. It is an instrument for song, and it is also the song itself. In this she is unique: she is herself a work of art. She is the magical being who makes music with her limbs.

9. The Myth

The art of ballet, so closely related as it is to the world of poetry
and dreams, deals with a different order of reality from that of
daily life. It might be argued that naturalism, or "realism" as
it is sometimes called, has little place in any work of art which
is essentially a formal structure, whether it be a novel, a poem
or a play. Indeed, it is ironical that one of the foremost advo-
cates of naturalism in the novel and drama, Emile Zola, in fact
produced works as highly selective of material and carefully
structured as any of those of his derided predecessors. In the
same way, when Robert Helpmann created his ballet, *Miracle in
the Gorbals*, in 1944 he received much acclaim for bringing the
problems of modern life—in this case the viciousness and
squalor of a Glasgow slum—into the rarefied world of the
ballet. In fact he had done nothing of the kind: *Miracle in the
Gorbals*, in its juxtaposition of solo dances and *pas de deux*
against the movements of the *corps de ballet*, was as intricately
designed as any of its predecessors. It was a piece of theatrical
artifice not a social document, and, as a result, it was praised
for quite the wrong reasons. Its fault was that, while it sought
for naturalism by mimicking natural movement and gesture, it
failed to translate these into dance images, so that the effect was
weakened and sentimentalised.

The reality for which one seeks in the ballet is deeper than
this, having its roots in the myths, legends and allegories whose
beginnings are lost in the dawn of time, yet which we inherit in
the total world of our unconscious life. They are the eternal

springs of art, because they are an aspect of our own being, those memories we carry in our blood. The dance, as we have seen, arose out of ritual, at first in the pagan rites to invoke or pacify the gods, and was then incorporated into the early religious rites of pre-Christian and Christian civilisations. It is with their great primal themes that the ballet is truly concerned; even from the first myth, told to us in Genesis, when God separated the light from the darkness, establishing the profound duality of life that is the primary source of all drama. In John Wain's fine phrase, the dance is concerned with "sculptures in metaphor" so as to reach the springs of our hidden life. This central feature of the dance is well put by Lewis Spence in his book *Myth and Ritual in Dance, Game and Rhyme*, when he writes:

> Ritual, dance and myth are really one: they were originally individual parts of a single thought-process, and only in course of time did they come to possess a separate existence of their own, as magical acts, fictions, dances, by which time they had lost something of their first significance as the composite part of a co-ordinate process. Ritual . . . remains as the ghostly mother of all the arts . . .

This ancient source of its inspiration still belongs to the ballet, more closely so than with any other art, because the dance is the primary expression of human emotion, whether in a tribal ritual or in a great *pas de deux* of classical ballet. For they spring from a single root, and speak to us of great mysteries. As Lucian says in his *Peri Orcheseos*: "You cannot find a single ancient mystery in which there is not dancing . . . Many people say of those who reveal the mysteries that they dance them out." This is true today as it was in the first century, and it remains central to the art of ballet.

One can observe most clearly in the classical ballet of the past the shaping of the myth. This is the central feature of works both in the classic and romantic tradition, including *Swan Lake* and *The Sleeping Beauty* at one extreme, and *Giselle* and *La Sylphide* at the other. Here the *danseur noble* occupies the central position, where through his eyes we see the unfolding of the drama. These ballets are essentially the story of a quest, and as such explore the same myth as the great allegories of many cultures and different ages. The male dancer is the central figure that we find in *The Odyssey*, *Moby Dick*, *The Faerie Queene*, *Everyman*, *Peer Gynt* or *The Pilgrim's Progress*. It is through him we watch the progress of his journey, during which he suffers many experiences and enters many perils, before he reaches his journey's end, and discovers the purpose of his voyaging. Albrecht seeks for the spirit of his dead Giselle in the mysterious forest, as Sigfried searches for Odette at the Lakeside, or the Prince journeys to the secret palace of the Sleeping Princess. James follows the phantom of the Sylphide to the fantastic glade, near the cavern of the witch; like Giselle, Odette and the vision of Aurora, she is the illusiory ideal, the dream that haunts him, and in pursuit of which he can never rest. At the end, like Pilgrim or Red Cross, they achieve their dream, even if, like Albrecht and James, it fades away as they grasp it. The classical ballets are thus heroic allegories of the human spirit, and it is due to this, as much as to the beauty of their music and choreography, that they survive into our own time.

As well as a quest, they are also allegories of the eternal conflict between good and evil, between darkness and light. Odile and von Rothbart in *Swan Lake* are exactly paralleled by Duessa and Archimago in *The Faerie Queene*; each is what Spenser called "a dark conceit", and it was fascinating to observe in Frederick Ashton's ballet, *The Quest* (a retelling of the same myth), how the role of Duessa was played by Beryl Grey with the same malevolence and dark duplicity as her Odile, making us aware how both choreographer and ballerina saw these two characters as mirror-images of one another. The same figures of evil can be found in Carabosse in *The Sleeping Beauty*, Madge, the witch, in *La Sylphide* and Myrtha, the Queen of the Wilis, in *Giselle*. The central drama in all these ballets is this struggle, expressed in a pursuit of the ideal. This is particularly well brought out in Eva Evdokimova's superb interpretation of Odette in Beryl Grey's production of *Swan Lake* for the Festival Ballet, where, in one agonised moment, Odette is seen torn between the conflicting wills of Sigfried and

Von Rothbart, so that her whole, trembling body is racked by a sudden anguish as she stands powerless between them, at the exact position of balance between two opposing forces. The same image may be observed in Natalia Makarova's sublime enactment of the Second Act of *Giselle*, when she is drawn from the protection of the Cross by Myrtha, leaving, with a pitiful reluctance, her beloved Albrecht to stand alone. The whole of the great poem of this Act is formed out of the struggle between Myrtha and Giselle for the soul of Albrecht, and in its triumphant conclusion, and in the music also, we reach the victory of good over evil, expressed symbolically by the light of the gathering dawn.

The settings of the classical ballets are in a timeless, secret world lit by no known sun but by the purer light of the imagination. They are at once divorced from ordinary life and are also an expression of that life as seen in dreams, full of the same mysterious revelations and strange insights. It is an enclosed, magical world like that of the walled garden in the thirteenth-century legend, *The Romance of the Rose*, and, indeed, these ballets express many of the same ideals of courtly love that were first established by the Troubadour poets of the eleventh century. The ballerina stands for the ideal love, for ever chaste and unapproachable, who belongs to those distant romances and to the poetry of the nineteenth century. She is the pursued, but never possessed; the loved, who is never attained. This sense of romantic yearning has been immortally expressed by Keats in the opening stanza of *La Belle Dame Sans Merci*:

> O what can ail thee, knight-at-arms,
> Alone and palely loitering?
> The sedge has withered from the lake,
> And no birds sing.

We find, too, in *Swan Lake* this same vision in the solo of the Prince, now a part of the first act in several productions. It expresses the loneliness, the longing for love, the emptiness in the heart that is so commonly suffered by the heroes of romantic poetry. Both Sigfried and the Prince in *The Sleeping Beauty* reject the offers of a human love—in Sigfried's case when he dismisses all his potential brides in the ballroom scene, and with the Prince when he abandons his lady companion, and rather brusquely too, during the forest scene, choosing instead to be alone with his solitary brooding from which springs the vision of Aurora and the Lilac Fairy.

The beautiful and ancient symbol of the rose as a token of human love is exquisitely embroidered into the ballet in Petipa's choreography for the *rose adagio* where the ballerina accepts a rose from each of her four partners. The rose, in the sweet brevity of its flowering, is also a symbol of the fleeting nature of youth and love, where joy has no more permanence than a rose; thus the *adagio* foreshadows the false promise of this dawn, to be ended by the malignancy of Carabosse, a figure both of age and death, beneath whose spell Aurora sinks into her enchanted sleep. This aspect of the ballet is wonderfully expressed by William Drummond of Hawthornden in his poem *Urania*:

> Ah! When I had what most I did admire,
> And saw of life's delights the last extremes,
> I found all but a rose hedged with a briar,
> A naught, a thought, a show of mocking dreams.

The Sleeping Beauty is a ballet of warmth, of the bright summer air. It has something of the dazzling brilliance of *As You Like It* where the sun dances between the lines and shimmers between each phrase. It is, therefore, appropriate that its central symbol should be the rose, the flower that above all others glows in its own fire and holds within it all the radiance of summer. To it is added this sense of impermanence, the ending of the long bright day. In his famous lyric Edmund Waller has expressed this finally and for all time:

> Then die—that she
> The common fate of all things rare
> May read in thee;
> How small a part of time they share
> That are so wondrous sweet and fair!

The use of the flower motif is here so different from that of *Giselle*: there the flowers are icy night blooms, cold from the chill of the tomb, spectral blossoms grown above a grave. It is in the use of such timeless symbols that the art of classical ballet is at one with that of poetry, for each explores reality at a far more profound level than any we know in the common light of day. The words of a poem are like dancers as they move along the musical line, articulating the silence that opens out between each phrase.

There is a strange duality in the attitude of the romantic poets to the role of woman: at one extreme she is seen as a distant, unattainable beauty, while at the other, she is envisaged as a destroyer, the bringer of evil and death, whom she so often personifies. This duality is, of course, symbolised in the double nature of Odette and Odile, and it is not solely for technical reasons that the roles are played by the same ballerina. It can also be seen in many modern works, the greatest of which is the Roland Petit/Cocteau ballet, *Le Jeune Homme et la Mort*. Thus in both works of the nineteenth century and in those of today, the ballerina is still portrayed either as Duessa or Una, either as Aldonza or Dulcinea, as temptress or ideal.

These same myths are found in the works of modern choreographers of many different schools. Frederick Ashton, for example, has used the idea of the quest not only in his ballet of that title, but also in earlier works like *The Wanderer* and *Apparitions*, while the struggle between good and evil is explicitly stated in his *Dante Sonata* in the conflict between the Children of Light and the Children of Darkness, as it is also in *Horoscope*, dealing with the struggle between the followers of Leo and those of Gemini. In the same way, the image of woman as one who destroys as she is loved, is the central drama of Ninette de Valois' *Checkmate* which, in the Prologue, is portrayed as a struggle between love and death. The myth must not, therefore, be considered as something antique or irrelevant to our times, for it is central to all human experience, and probably will always be so.

An important feature of the great literary allegories is the contrast between the world of dream and that of reality. Indeed they are sometimes seen as a dream, in which the realities of everyday are incorporated and woven into the same fabric.

The famous opening to *The Pilgrim's Progress* establishes this duality at once:

> As I walked through the wilderness of this world, I lighted on a certain place where was a Den, and I laid me down in that place to sleep: and, as I slept, I dreamed a dream. I dreamed, and behold, I saw a man clothed with rags, standing in a certain place, with his face from his own house, a book in his hand, and a great burden upon his back. I looked and saw him open the book and read therein; and, as he read, he wept, and trembled; and not being able longer to contain, he broke out with a lamentable cry, saying, "What shall I do?"

In the same manner the ballets of the nineteenth century work on these two levels. In *Swan Lake* is contrasted the world of the royal garden and palace against the magical lake-side; in *The Sleeping Beauty* we find the contrast between the palace and the wood where the Prince sees the vision of Princess Aurora. Despite its foolish libretto, *Casse-Noisette* is set within a dream, where the Kingdom of the Snow provides its own dream-landscape. *Giselle* shows us the clearing in the forest where Giselle lives, and, in the second act, the haunted wood where she is buried and where the ghostly wilis dance their secret rites. The pattern is very similar in *La Sylphide* where the realistic setting of the first act is offset by the dream world into which James is let in pursuit of the Sylphide. And it is more than just a matter of the placing of a scene; the contrast in the style of dancing indicates very clearly the different aspects of the two dimensions, where the purest classical style is used in the dream sequences, while those set in the realistic world will incorporate folk court and peasant dances within them.

As he enters upon his search, the hero of the allegory finds himself in a haunted place, often a wood or a forest to emphasise this aspect of darkness and mystery. The immortal opening lines of *The Divine Comedy* (in Laurence Binyon's translation) brings to mind at once the dark and evil wood of the second act of *Giselle*:

> Midway the journey of this life I was 'ware
> That I had strayed into a dark forest,

The Myth

And the right path appeared not anywhere.
Ah, tongue cannot describe how it oppressed,
This wood, so harsh, dismal and wild, that fear
At thought of it strikes now into my breast.

It cannot be purely coincidental that, in the classic ballets of the past, the setting for the scenes of fantasy and dream all take place in a wood, held enchanted by spirits from another world. It is the darkness through which the journeying man must travel to find his own peace, and it is in peace and reconciliation that *Giselle, Swan Lake* and *The Sleeping Beauty* end, whether it is found in this life, or whether in death, beyond the dark wood.

The idea of rebirth is central to the myth. Indeed it might well be considered the basic theme of art as well as life, seen as much in the ceaseless rhythms of the seasons as in the most fundamental beliefs of mankind from his earliest imaginings to the Christian doctrine of the Resurrection. This myth is expressed on two levels in *The Sleeping Beauty*: in the rebirth of nature and the coming of Spring, established when the Prince sails down the river of dreams where the scenery changes to the pattern of the seasons, and in the human story of a girl's awakening to love. The ancient myth of the Spring kissing the dead year to wakefulness is also incorporated into the legend, and it is customary to set the dream sequence in the wood during autumn or winter, so that the Prince's kiss may include this symbolism.

Even her name, Aurora, contains the symbolism of the ballet, for it is concerned with the dawning of love as it is of the awakening of the earth. In her enchanted sleep Aurora has passed from childhood to that of a woman in love; so also the winter sleep of the earth promises the dawn of Spring. The rose, symbol of love, that is offered to her in the great *adagio* of Act I, spreads in the final act its opened petals, as we see them in the unfolding of her limbs.

So also the love between Odette and Sigfried that he betrays to Odile is re-born in the apotheosis where the lovers are re-united in death. Here not only is the myth of re-birth, but also that of the triumph of good over evil which is so often incor-

89

porated within it. In order to conform with Soviet orthodoxy, producers of versions of *Swan Lake* for the Bolshoi and Kirov companies have been forced to give the ballet a happy ending, where only one aspect of the myth is shown, thus robbing the ballet of any deeper spiritual significance. This, of course, is a betrayal of the choreography, but it is no doubt impossible for Soviet producers of the ballet to fight against a tyranny of this nature.

In *Giselle* also, the rebirth of the love of Giselle and Albrecht is found beyond the grave, where again the victory of the forces of good over evil is won. Here they have achieved their reconciliation through grief and suffering, and this is a common feature of allegory, where the hero has to undergo many griefs in order to attain his ideal. Albrecht kills Giselle by his betrayal, Sigfried wounds Odette by his own and each grows in stature, maturity and understanding because of this; they are, in T. S. Eliot's words:

> . . . restored by that refining fire
> Where you must move in measure, like a dancer.

The stories of the classic ballets are those where the spirit is refined in this way by suffering to achieve an inner reconciliation. After the winter is come the Spring, symbolised in the reconciliation of two hearts. This is clearly seen in *Giselle* and *Swan Lake*, and is indeed, the central theme of both ballets. In *The Sleeping Beauty* the symbolism is here on a much more superficial level, since the character of the Prince is an empty one; he appears for this first time quite late in the ballet, and is drawn without any depth. The story, on a human level, is concerned with the Princess Aurora, rather than her prince. However most producers will make clear the importance of the section of the ballet, as does Tchaikovsky with some of his greatest music, where the Prince journeys to find Aurora. He fights and defeats the evil Carabosse and her attendant spirits, struggles through brambles, undergrowth and thickets of trees to attain the magical place. It is, indeed, only in this section of the ballet that the myth of the achievement of love through suffering is fully expressed, and it is unfortunate that some producers treat it as a kind of interlude and occasionally omit it completely.

In the symbolism of the classical ballet we thus observe the pattern of our inner world expressed in visible form. As Coleridge has put it:

> We may safely define allegorical writing as the employment of one set of agents and images with actions and accompaniments correspondent, so as to convey, while in disguise, either moral qualities or conceptions of the mind that are not in themselves objects of the senses, so that the difference is everywhere presented to the idea or imagination, while the likeness is suggested to the mind; and this connectedly so that the parts combine to form a consistent whole.

We can, therefore, appreciate the classical ballet on many different levels, each of which relate to one another to express the myth in both human and symbolic terms. Princess Aurora is any young girl growing up, any woman in love. She is also an ideal of romantic love. She is also a symbol of the awakening earth. It gives the ballet great depth and resonance to realise this, since these ideas are not exclusive of one another, but reflect and relate in a mysterious way. This is so in all great allegories. In *The Divine Comedy*, for example, Dante's Beatrice is a girl, a symbol of love, an image of Divine Grace. This aspect of what one might call multiple symbolism is described by Goethe as follows:

> Since we have many experiences that cannot be plainly expressed or communicated, I have long adopted the method of revealing the secret meaning to attentive readers by images that confront one another and are, so to speak, reflected in one another.

So it is not only with the symbolism of classical ballet, but also with the symbols of the classical dance. One is reminded of a remark of Mallarmé concerning the words of a poem, that they work "through reciprocal reflection, like the flash of fire over jewels".

I am not suggesting that all, or even most ballets are concerned with such great themes as I have been discussing. There is a place for comedy, for satire, for simple high spirits, and the word of ballet would be much impoverished without *Coppélia* and *La Fille mal Gardée*. It can also provide us with the delight in beautiful movement that carries no meaning beyond itself. Yet, at its highest, the ballerina must not forget that she is on the frontier of a great mystery that lies beyond the music as if behind a shimmering veil. For the dance is that "flash of fire", that moment's insight. It transcends words, as the music of a poem expresses more than the words that compose it. It is of our time, yet out of time. It will always remain a mystery.

10. *Classical and Romantic—I*

Two great ballets of the nineteenth century, *Swan Lake* and *Giselle*, dwarf the horizon, and all ballets composed in our time lie under their shadow. One cannot disregard them, nor pass them by, for they summarize the tradition of the art to which dancers and choreographers must return, as to the source of their inspiration. They embody many features of the myth, as I have discussed it in the previous chapter, and their symbolism remains as powerful today as it did a hundred years ago.

The myth of the Swan-maiden is one of the most ancient to survive down to our own times, and anthropologists have traced its beginnings as far back as the Bronze Age, where it is lost among the immemorial legends of mankind. It has belonged to many races and cultures; it is found in Scandinavian myths, in German folklore and in Celtic tales. The most common form of the myth describes a flock of swans arriving at a lake where they are transformed into girls who bathe naked in the waters. A man, who has been watching them secretly, steals the clothes of one of them whom he then claims as his bride. Of the many variants to this story is the one we know of as *Swan Lake* which, in its turn, seems to derive in part from an Indian myth in which the divine Urvasi deserted her husband, and he found her again in the form of a swan swimming on a lake. The idea that the lake has been formed from the tears of Odette's grandfather seems to have been taken directly from the story of Cycnus in Ovid's *Metamorphosis* (Book 7). It was also a common legend in distant times that the souls of the dead are reincarnated as birds. The Babylonians and Assyrians believed this, as did the Aztecs and the Australian aborigines. In parts of Russia it was believed that children who died returned to us as swallows, while in Brittany it was said that if they died unbaptised they returned as birds to the earth they had left so early and so unknown.

In the same way the owl, that von Rothbart chooses as his disguise, has long been accepted by mankind as a symbol of evil or death. Lady Macbeth, in one terrible image, refers to the owl as "the fatal bellman", and indeed we can hear the syllables clang and echo like the tolling of a passing bell. So, too, the owl is seen as an omen, a presage of disaster. Casca in *Julius Caesar* says:

> And yesterday the bird of night did sit,
> Even at noonday, upon the market-place,
> Hooting and shrieking.

Many legends of ancient curses that follow a family down the centuries have figured the owl as the harbinger of its return; even a writer as learned as John Ruskin could say in all sincerity: "Whatever wise people may say of them, I at least myself have found the owl's cry always prophetic of mischief to me." It is not surprising, therefore, that *Swan Lake*, dealing as it does in the conflict between two such ancient beings, should reach deep into the consciousness of its audience, and perhaps this is one of the several reasons why it has survived the passage of time and fashion and remains a valid legend to us in our own, more sophisticated and materialistic age.

It may be that the libretto of *Swan Lake* was also inspired by the story of Mikáilo Ivánovitch, a figure from a popular Russian ballad. Mikáilo saw a swan on a lake, and drew his bow to shoot her. At this she turns into a beautiful maiden, and tells him she is a heathen princess, and if he can arrange for her to be baptised, she will marry him. In a Hessian story the narrative remains the same, but, in this case, she could be freed from her enchantment if he would say a Paternoster for her every Sunday for twelve months. He agrees to do so, but fails and loses her forever.

It is very probable that the creators of *Swan Lake* also had in mind the poem of Pushkin, *Tale of the Tsar Saltan*, that contains a passage telling how the White Swan of Russian folklore is saved by the Prince from the wicked Hawk, to appear to him then in the guise of a beautiful woman.

It is a common feature of the myth of the enchanted princess that she is transformed by evil magic into an animal or bird. One version of this concerns the daughter of Hippocrates, the famous physician, who was said to have been enchanted by Diana on the island of Cos, and this has been described by William Morris in his poem "The Earthly Paradise":

> Then listen! When this day is overpast,
>   A fearful monster I shall be again.
> And thou may'st be my saviour at the last,
>   Unless, once more, thy words are nought and vain;
>   If thou of love and sovereignty art fain,
> Come thou next morn, and when thou seest here
> A hideous dragon, have thereof no fear,
>
> But take the loathsome head up in thine hands,
>   And kiss it, and be master presently
> Of twice the wealth that is in all the lands,
>   From Cathay to the head of Italy;
>   And master also, if it pleaseth thee,
> Of all thou praisest as so fresh and bright,
> Of what thou callest crown of all delight.
>
> "Ah me! to hold my child upon my knees,
> After the weeping of unkindly tears,
> And all the wrongs of these four hundred years."

Odette, the swan queen, thus clearly belongs to the same legends. She is also the ideal of feminine beauty that, as we have seen, had been taken over in the classical ballet from the ideas of courtly love of the middle ages. She is the distant enchantress, the ideal one. In a sense, as I mentioned in the previous chapter, the duality of attitude to woman down the ages, as either an ideal or a temptress, is perfectly imagined in the double nature of Odette and Odile, and it could be argued that the choreography suggests on one level that Sigfried embraces both as a single person, and that he is drawn by the ideal only to be betrayed by her darker nature. In either case he is enchanted, for there could be no other reason for him to succumb to the charms of Odile, since in all productions of the ballet, she is portrayed as vicious, cruel and loveless.

The male dancer, before whose eyes the myth is enacted, is essentially two-dimensional; he is more a spectator than a participant in his own drama, reacting to forces outside himself whose nature he little understands. Sigfried in *Swan Lake* is, at the beginning of the ballet, an immature, adolescent figure, dominated by his mother of whom he seems singularly afraid, and dependent upon male companionship and the guidance of his tutor. So far he is not a promising figure as the hero for a tale of courtly love, and would plainly be more interested in a night out with the boys than in any dreams of an ideal love. When he is told by his mother that he is obliged to choose a wife, his reaction is one of dismay, and he shows more delight when she gives him a present of the cross-bow. This has plainly embarrassed producers of the ballet who realise that Sigfried is a poor candidate for a romantic hero; indeed in the recent version by the Bolshoi Ballet, first seen in London in 1974, all reference to the cross-bow is omitted, so that he is drawn to the magical wood, not in order to shoot swans, but because of a secret yearning of his own. Many producers in recent years have also added a solo as in the Bolshoi version, to indicate Sigfried's loneliness and desire for love; in this way the vision of Odette may come to him as a figment of his solitary dreaming, a projection from his own heart.

There is much to be said for this approach, since it is far more consistent with the working of the myth. For otherwise, if the ballet is produced in the conventional manner of the past, Sigfried is seen as an ordinary, rather dull young man who is suddenly overtaken by a love he had never expected. He has encountered a vision, and he is, from that instant, enchanted. There must, I think, be some preparation for this, as there is in *The Sleeping Beauty*, where the Prince dismisses his companions and lapses into a trance of thought and brooding imagination, from which the image of Aurora springs. It is true Sigfried does the same, but only, it appears, because he wishes to continue the shoot alone; it seems a great deal more like selfishness than romantic grief, and ill prepares us for his immediate acceptance of Odette. For this reason, it is essential that Sigfried has either a solo dance or a passage of mime in the first act to establish him as a romantic hero; it is not sufficient just for him to look moody or bored at his party, since this only indicates bad manners rather than suppressed ardour.

In the pursuit of the ideal one transforms that ideal into the real and loved. It is on this psychological level that the symbolism of *Swan Lake* exists also. At his first sight of Odette, the Prince, in Stendhal's famous image, crystallized his emotions around her. He is in love, not with the real woman, but with his idea of her; she is a product of his lonely imaginings, a fantasy of his solitude. She is a symbol of love—not the loved one. It is this that gives *Swan Lake* its universal appeal, for most of us have, at one time or another, crystallized our emotions around a beloved object, and grown to love her in time as she truly is, even if we have to endure the disappointment of losing the ideal. In Jungian terms, Sigfried projects his emotions on to Odette. The story of the Second Act is the transformation of that love, the most common and most human of all our experiences.

From a more dynamic system of psychology, that of Alfred Adler, one might see the character of Sigfried as that of the man who uses his ideal or imagined love to avoid having to face the reality of a mortal and imperfect love. In this manner, Sigfried is able to reject all his future brides in Act III because none of them lives up to the ideal; he can, therefore, remain uncommitted with a good conscience. I have also seen an essay in which his character was studied in Freudian terms of the working of the Oedipus Complex, but this merely seems to be an attempt to explain one myth by means of another, and certainly not very helpful.

Not only, therefore, is Ivanov's choreography of the Second Act of *Swan Lake* a superlative example of poetic design, it also embodies a double theme of the struggle between good and

D

evil, between love and death, together with that of the pursuit of the ideal, that is, as we have seen, central to all great allegories. Some producers make a mistake in disregarding this and underplaying the role of Von Rothbart in the guise of an owl. In this form he stands as the bringer of death, a symbol of metaphysical evil, and much of the drama of this Act is concerned with his struggle with Sigfried for the possession of Odette who, like Una in *The Faerie Queene* or Beatrice in *The Divine Comedy*, is the spirit of truth and incorruptible beauty. Here indeed is the classic encounter between dark and light, the primal myth of all mankind. In this respect *Swan Lake* expresses the same theme that is found in the Second Act of *Giselle*, where the Queen of the Wilis and Giselle fight for the soul of Albrecht, making each of these works similar products of the Romantic imagination, where the difference between the Romantic and Classical, so often made between them, is seen to be without foundation.

Observed in this light, the Second Act of *Swan Lake* contains a profound spiritual truth, for it is concerned with the redemption of Odette from the dark kingdom of death into the world of light. It is, in this respect, not dissimilar to *The Sleeping Beauty* that deals in the same symbols of rebirth. If the possession of Odette by von Rothbart were ever to be completely achieved, she would become Odile, the personification of evil, and it is that evil Sigfried is tempted to embrace in the Third Act. He is, in fact, a man drawn by two images, of good and of evil, and his anguish is that, for a time, he is unable to distinguish between them. Thus *Swan Lake* can be considered in a spiritual light in the same tradition as *The Pilgrim's Progress* and *Everyman*. Sigfried is an universal figure—the searcher for truth, the man that is tempted, falls and is redeemed by the power of love. This echoes, of course, the Christian drama of the Fall and the Redemption, and gives to *Swan Lake* a profundity of meaning far beyond that of a charming fairy story, as it is so often treated both by producers and critics.

In various productions attempts have been made to rationalize the symbolism of the work, but I feel this has been due to a misunderstanding of the nature of symbolism. The strength of the allegory exists precisely because it can be explained at different levels, and can be approached from many different angles; it is more a search for truth than a logical explanation of that truth, containing within it all the strange logic of dreams. Kenneth MacMillan, in his production for his Berlin Company, presented the story as if it were the Prince's dream, from which at the end he awakens to his true love. This is an interesting approach, but it weakens the effect of the allegory in which the dream, as with that of Pilgrim, is in fact his reality, his true world. In John Cranko's production for the Stuttgart Ballet the Prince dies alone, leaving Odette for ever as a swan, but this provides no resolution to the allegory and leaves it half-developed: in the pursuit of truth the hero of allegory must find it and grasp it otherwise there is no purpose to his adventure, no universal meaning.

The richness of symbolism embodied in the character of Odette was (in my experience, for the first time) revealed in Natalia Makarova's incomparable interpretation of the role with the Royal Ballet in 1972. This great dancer, supreme exponent of classicism in our age, found within the character of Odette a depth of meaning undisclosed to her predecessors. Makarova showed us the double nature of Odette as both swan and woman existing together in the same person, so bringing out the swan motifs, so clearly expressed in Ivanov's choreography. One realized then that there is no other way of dealing with this central problem of the role, for to treat Odette as a woman who is released from her bondage of a swan between the night hours, is to make nonsense both of the choreography and the legend. Indeed, in an otherwise excellent book on choreography, the authors express the view that the top half of Odette is a swan and the bottom half a woman (or *vice versa*), thus reducing the myth to such a level of bathos it is a wonder they ever bothered to see it in the theatre at all.

We must not forget that Odette is a poetic image, and like all images includes several different aspects of truth, held together within a central design. There is both a multiplicity and an ambiguity in poetic symbolism, as has been explored by William Empson in his book, *Seven Types of Ambiguity*, and the character of Odette is a complete example of this. She is a woman and a swan; both aspects of her nature, which one might describe as the instinctive and the rational, exist together. She is both a wild creature and a woman in love. In Makarova's interpretation, at her first entry Odette is shown in the grip of an instinctive terror at the approach of a human being, but as the relationship between her and Sigfried develops, particularly during the great *pas de deux*, her humanity begins to emerge into the light, as the spirit of love searches for it. The woman, hidden within the swan, begins slowly to emerge, just as the choreography develops the bird movements into those of the pure classical ballerina, until, by the end of this Act, the transformation is complete: the creature of instinct is replaced by the woman in love; by love she has been redeemed and restored to her humanity. This is the profound truth about *Swan Lake*, revealed to us at last, free from obscurity, in the performance of one great dancer. She has shown us how love can tame and humanize instinctive nature, and draw the human spirit from all its dark disguises.

There is no contradiction in this multiplicity of images, for they explore reality at several different levels—the spiritual, the psychological and the universal. Truth in art has many facets; it glitters, like a diamond, through the refraction of these surfaces one on another, so that it achieves that "flash of fire" Mallarmé found in the imagery of a poem.

I have never seen a satisfactory production of the Third Act of *Swan Lake*. In a previous book, *The Ballerina*, I maintained that it is necessary to restore to it a sense of dark Gothic romance, made easier if one accepts Odile (as Cyril Beaumont has pointed out) as von Rothbart's familiar spirit. She is to Sigfried no more real than was Odette at his first sight of her; she is the spirit of evil that tempts and finally destroys him. Petipa's choreography superbly echoes the swan movements of Odette, giving to them sharp and brutal outlines, and unless audiences are aware of this sense of identity between the two characters, emphasized by the fact that they are danced by the same ballerina, Sigfried merely appears to be a gullible fool, taken in by an obvious and banal deception, so that they lose all sym-

100

pathy with him and reduce his stature as a romantic hero, the pivot of the entire allegory. One must realise that Sigfried sees another aspect of Odette in the figure of Odile; his betrayal is not that he takes a vow to love Odile, but that he is capable of loving what he thinks of as base in Odette. He has betrayed his ideal, and in doing so, he has betrayed himself. In a sense, he has fallen from grace; only by suffering and repentance, seen in the final Act, can he be redeemed, and then only beyond the grave. In order to deceive others, we must first deceive ourselves and this is what Sigfried has done.

It is therefore not sufficient to portray Odile as a vicious, ill-natured tart, smirking at Von Rothbart behind her hand. She must be seen as his creation, and it should not be beyond the ingenuity of some future producer to make her dance only at Von Rothbart's bidding, as if her dance were a mirror image of his own gestures. Also it would heighten the drama and the central symbolism of this Act, were the Prince's mother and other members of the Court allowed to see through this deception and seek, by every means, to wake Sigfried from his evil dream. For Odile is beautiful and enticing to Sigfried only; his mother and his companions are like the audience, and they can see how easily he is deceived. There seems to me no reason why Odette herself should not make her first entry with Von Rothbart. Of course the part would have to be played by another dancer, but she could enter on *pas de bourrée*, which is how Sigfried last saw her, even with her back to the audience, only then to re-emerge as Odile. It does not seem to me sufficient that the ghostly image of Odette should be projected behind the dancers, and to be seen pleading with Sigfried; it is necessary to go further, to emphasise how close Odile is in appearance and manner to Odette, perhaps in the same way as Robert Helpmann in his ballet, *Hamlet*, expressed the confusion in Hamlet's mind between his mother and Ophelia, showing both dancers in a kind of double image. However this is done, we must not destroy the high seriousness of *Swan Lake* by empty virtuosity or crude melodrama: there is more to Act III than setting the house aroar.

In the great tradition of the classical dance *Swan Lake* is its huge supporting arch, central to its structure and its design. It represents the meeting point of the romantic and classical tradition, where Ivanov's two Acts are a triumph of sensibility, and Pepita's are the achievements of logic and reason. They represent the double aspect of creativity in art to which Valéry referred as the work of "the cool scientist" and "the subtle dreamer". From Ivanov's creation were to spring the ballets of Fokine and Tudor and the latter day classicism of Vaganova-trained dancers at the Kirov school in Leningrad, where the classical dance has reached its highest peak of expressiveness; from Petipa's were to grow the ballets of pure design and formal movement of Balanchine and Ashton. In the merging of these two styles lies the future of the classical dance whose forerunners can perhaps be seen in the works of van Manen and Tetley, where great plasticity of movement is combined with a formal precision of style. *Swan Lake* is not only a summary of what had up to that time been achieved in the classical dance in the works of Bournonville, Perrot and Vigano, it is also the source of future development in the art: here, at the meeting point of past and future, stands this immortal work, indifferent to the changes of fashion, unassailed by time or time's decay.

11. Classical and Romantic—II

To move back half a century from the ideas of *Swan Lake* to those of *Giselle* is to find ourselves in a known world, lit by a more familiar light than that of Petipa's and Ivanov's strange allegory. For here is a human love, the story of its betrayal and its reconciliation beyond the grave. It is near to us as love, as grief, near to us, yet far away in the strange haunted world of the Romantic imagination.

In his fine study, *The Ballet Called Giselle*, Cyril Beaumont investigates in great detail the origin of the work and the different parts played in this by its various collaborators. He concludes that most of the choreography for *Giselle* is the creation of Perrot inspired by his mistress, Carlotta Grisi, for whom he wished to find a suitable role to establish her at the Opéra, while the narrative and the mime scenes in the first Act were created by Coralli, then resident choreographer. When the ballet was revived by Petipa in the late nineteenth century at St Petersburg, he amended the choreography in certain details and created the *grand pas* for the Wilis that opens the Second Act. Petipa had worked with Perrot at the Maryinsky, and it is undoubtedly true that he was deeply influenced by Perrot's ideas of the dance as an expression of emotion and atmosphere that he was to take over in his greatest ballet, *The Sleeping Beauty*, which is a study in character as much as in the formal style.

No great work of the imagination can have had so frivolous an inspiration as *Giselle*. Gautier, after reading *De l'Allemagne*, which contains a passage relating to the story of the Wilis, concluded: "Wouldn't this make a pretty ballet!" Gautier was essentially a dilettante, despite the fact that he was also a very considerable writer, and his interest in the ballet was essentially superficial; he was not truly concerned with it either as a composite art or an exploration into the nature of poetic truth that were to absorb both Valéry and Mallarmé in the future. It seems he left the First Act to the librettist Saint-Georges, being only worried by the "pretty death" (as he described it) that had to be invented for Giselle. Gautier's interest was concentrated on the Second Act, during which his obsession with vampirism and the Fatal Woman was satisfied in the creation of Myrtha, Queen of the Wilis, whose character and relationship between Albrecht and Giselle has been little studied by writers on the ballet.

Beaumont tells us that the legend of the Wilis is of Slavonic origin, and that the word Wili is derived from *vila* (plural *vile*) meaning vampire. As Mario Praz points out in his famous book, *The Romantic Agony*, a curiosity about vampires was an abiding feature of the Romantic Age, and this can be found in the works of Byron, Poe, Gautier, Baudelaire and Flaubert among others. To this must be added their obsession with woman as a bringer of death and corruption that is found continually in novels and poems of that time. The theme of the betrayal of innocence also held an abiding fascination for writers of the Romantic era, deeply influenced as they were by Samuel Richardson's vast novel, *Clarissa*, and Laclos' *Les Liaisons Dangereuses*.

We can see, therefore, how deeply *Giselle* mirrored the central beliefs of the age to an even greater extent than its precursor, *La Sylphide*. Nor have its themes a purely period flavour, since they are a common feature of our own time, as they were also of the distant past. Woman as the destroyer, the bringer of evil, is a concept that goes back to the legend of the Garden of Eden, and it is to be found also in the Greek myths where Althaea murders her own son, Scylla murders her father and Clytemnestra murders her husband. The destruction of innocence is the central theme in the plays of Jean Anouilh today, as it is the basis of many novels by Graham Greene.

These two ideas, symbolised in *Giselle* by the characters of Giselle herself and Myrtha, Queen of the Wilis, provide the ballet with its central conflict, the ancient struggle between good and evil, that we have observed also in *Swan Lake*, thus showing both works in the common light of the romantic imagination.

Giselle is a ballet of autumn and winter—the autumn of a dying love, the winter of the grave. There is no summer in it, no spring. The dark comes early: the sound of the hunting horns are in its music of farewell. Autumn is, of course, the time for parting—the leaf from the tree and all the green of summer burnt away; it is inescapable as the fading light, the thrust of a bleak wind suddenly out of the darkness. There is a cruel irony in this—that the story of young love should be set in such a time, when each kiss is not a greeting, but a valediction, a farewell.

This undercurrent of sadness, of impending loss, symbolised in autumn trees, must be seen to permeate the atmosphere of the First Act, and be a constant presence in the interpretation of the title role. In his use of *leit-motivs* and a hint of concealed menace in his score, Adolphe Adam underlines this: the Wilis are not ever far away, and their dance is heard to move secretly beneath the music.

It is in the few minutes after her first entry that the ballerina must thus establish the character of Giselle, and here she faces one of the greatest challenges of Romantic art. She has to create, with very small means at her disposal, a portrait of the doomed innocent that has always been one of the most touching figures of Romanticism, and has, at the same time, to make it clear for us that she is of such a nature that it would take little to drive her mad. This was the achievement of Anna Pavlova and Olga Spessivtzeva, as it was of Alicia Markova near our own time; today it is a secret known to one ballerina only, Natalia Makarova, who has found it in the music and in the depth of her own heart.

Who was Giselle? We know no more than that she was a peasant girl. Certainly she seems to have lived a strange life, away from her companions in the fields, sheltered by her mother, excluded from all in a clearing in the wood. She is nervous, highly strung, given to abrupt changes of mood, bursts of happiness, moments of sudden foreboding. It seems she has realised that Albrecht is not the peasant boy he pretends to be; if she did not think of him in some way her superior, come from a higher station in life, why then does she curtsy to where she believes he is hiding when first they meet? Perhaps she knows all along who he is: it is only through her imagination that she lets herself be deceived, chooses a game of love, another fantasy to comfort her in her solitude. She cannot face a real love, that of Hilarion; her feelings for Albrecht are a means of escape, a hint of her oncoming madness. Why do her companions crown her as Queen of the Vintage unless it is that they wish to reassure her, make her lose her sense of isolation from them all? Or is it, perhaps, that they recognise she comes from a different world than their own, is a foundling, whose father's name is unknown to them? It is better that we are left with such ambiguities, for, like the Chosen Virgin in *The Rite of Spring* she is the one who is doomed, even in the instant of her first meeting with Albrecht. Maybe that is why she snatches with such a fevered gaiety at each moment's joy; maybe she knows how little time remains, even as the autumn sun goes down to evening, on that last brief day of her love.

Albrecht is far indeed from being the traditional romantic hero; indeed he is little more than a philandering aristocrat, engaged in a passing infatuation with a village girl. Male dancers (who are not always the most modest of artists) have done their best to try and soften this unpleasant outline, that shows them in such an unfavourable light, by stressing the depth and sincerity of Albrecht's guilt and repentance in the Second Act. This has sometimes been carried to extremes as in the interpretation, for example, of Serge Lifar, where his paroxysms of grief were more inclined to embarrass the audience than to touch their hearts. The finest portrait, in my experience, was that of George Skibine, who made no attempt to sentimentalise the character: in his version, Albrecht was both frivolous, insincere and cruel; for him the encounter with Giselle was solely a matter of a charming flirtation with an odd little girl whom it would interest him to seduce. It seems to me that if the moral concern of the First Act is with betrayal, the theme of the Second is that of repentance, and a heartless interpretation of Albrecht in fact heightens the contrast both dramatically and on a deeper, spiritual level.

If the First Act of *Giselle* belongs to the dancer *terre à terre*, whose immortal prototype is Fanny Elssler, the Second Act is designed for the dancer of *élévation*, of whom Marie Taglioni is the supreme representative. It therefore shows us the complete range of the classical ballerina as it has been developed over a hundred years, and there are few dancers indeed who are at home in both worlds, since they must be explored in two very different styles of dance which is a feat beyond the range of most ballerinas, however eminent. There have been great interpretations of the First Act from those of Tamara Karsavina to Margot Fonteyn; there have been many of the Second, including those of Alicia Markova, Yvette Chauviré and Ekaterina Maximova: today, in the performance of Natalia Makarova, we can see that rare and sublime reconciliation between them both.

The poetry of the Second Act lies not only in the exquisite balance of the choreography, but also in the manner in which the ghost of Giselle assumes a palpable reality, being at first little more than a figment of Albrecht's imagination and tortured conscience. When Albrecht first sees her it is as an outline formed by the swaying mist as it rises from the night. Shaped like the ghost of his lost girl, it dissolves and floats away, sketching a movement on the air, like the curve of her arms. She fades as the mist thins until she is no more than a wisp, a haze of light melting into the darkness.

It must feel to him that all his invocations, all his night's orisons, will never give being to this illusion, imprinted by a chance design on the air, with no more substance than the wind that formed those imagined arms, set a coronet of flowers on her brow. To dream that she had returned, and then to know it was nothing—a trick of the night wind—how absolute must have been his desolation, how total his solitude, alone now in the dark, besieged only by the ghost of memory, that most terrible of all our hauntings, the last and most cruel phantom that can never be laid to rest.

The repetition of various steps of the dance and phrases of music between the First and Second Acts of *Giselle* makes the Second Act a kind of echo of what has gone before, shadowed now not by the autumnal sun but by the ghost of the unseen moon. Certain passages of the dance rest within the phrase of music that encloses them, so that the music has assumed a visible shape within our memory. Thus, when we hear this music again and see those steps repeated within a setting that is the dark shadow of the earlier day, they form a kind of double image, ironic in all its terrible beauty, like the skull shaped beneath the living flesh. The steps to which Giselle danced in her happiness return, when danced by her ghostly companions, haunted by echos. *Giselle* is composed of such sad ironies, as when the dance itself which was her greatest joy is made the instrument that is chosen to kill the man she loves. So too, the images of flowers, most ancient symbol both of love and of the dying of such love, which are used in the First Act to test that love and later to garland her brow, are, in the Second Act, the symbol of her grief, her falling tears.

The opening dance of Giselle is fevered, trance-like; she turns unwilled, lifeless as a dead leaf caught in the desolate air. There is no hope in her, no love; only the memory of a grave, the sudden awakening to the cold earth. She turns as if she would never cease; then she begins to be aware of her own being, so that she breaks from the opening pose, spins, then begins to dance as she wills it, crosses the stage in great leaps, to disappear into the forest.

At first the power of the Queen of the Wilis over her is absolute: Giselle moves only at her bidding, but slowly, even in this transition during the first dance, one sees Myrtha's power begin to weaken and the conflict between the two beings intensify. It is not at once possible for Myrtha to draw Giselle from the safety of the Cross, or from Albrecht whose arms are held outstretched, so that he also stands in the figure of a cross; there is a tension, a sense of huge reluctance in the music when Giselle is called forward to begin the unsupported *adagio*—those sublime poses growing out of the stillness like the image of a sigh.

In his fine production for the Royal Ballet, Peter Wright makes here, in my view, one important misjudgment. In his version, when Giselle is drawn from the protection of the Cross, where she and Albrecht have sought sanctuary, he begins to follow her, and she gestures him to return. This allows the ballerina no opportunity to make clear that she is forced away by Myrtha from the Cross, and that, at this moment in the ballet, she is quite powerless.

The extreme cruelty of Myrtha is not just that she tries to force Albrecht to dance to his death, but that she uses her power over Giselle to bring this about. It is Giselle who leads Albrecht in the dance, even while she pleads with Myrtha to release her hold over them both. Giselle is totally bound. She is Myrtha's creature; only by the power of her love for Albrecht will she be able not only to save him but to release herself also, and the Second Act is, in part, the search for this freedom for them both. As this Act progresses Giselle begins to gain more and more freedom from her submission to Myrtha, so that towards the end she is able to beg her to relent, which would not be possible in her earlier, trance-like state. The dawn marks her victory; it is a light which, in Peter Wright's production, is most touchingly expressed in the manner the Wilis try to shade their eyes from the glare, for they are dazzled by it, this victory of love over the powers of darkness.

Now Giselle stretches out her arms towards Albrecht, wills with all her spent being that he shall live. The dawn breaks, marked by the chiming of a distant clock and the darkness lessens. When Myrtha and her companions withdraw, Giselle approaches Albrecht, and the music mounts to a climax both elegiac and triumphant. She stands behind him, her pose the still centre of this radiant music. It is her dawn, the victory of her perfect love. No invocation from beyond the grave will ever draw her from her sleep again: she has achieved her rest.

So the great poem of the Second Act of *Giselle* ends, in the perfect reconciliation, not only of art but of our divided human nature. The ballet remains one of the great monuments to the Romantic movement, this ghost from the past that beckons to us out of those shadows where dancers still discover the secrets of their mysterious art.

12. Contemporary Ballet

The two most powerful influences on the development of the classical dance over the past fifty years have been the rediscovery of Noverre's *Lettres sur la Danse et les Ballets*, first published in 1760, and the publication of Michel Fokine's manifesto in a letter to *The Times* on 6th July, 1914. To these must be added the first appearance of the Diaghilev Ballet in Paris in 1909 and the dominating influence of that Company over the next twenty years until the death of Diaghilev in 1929. It is to these ideas and to this Company that the dance in the Western world is largely indebted, though the debt has now been paid, and, one suspects, overpaid by the ballet companies that grew from this common source.

Noverre saw the ballet as a branch of drama, in which the dance had to acquire the same range of expressiveness and emotional content as the lines in a play, and the dancer develop as an interpretative artist in exactly the same manner as the actor. He puts his case with great trenchancy in his first Letter:

A ballet is a picture, or rather a series of pictures connected one with the other by the plot which provides the theme of the ballet; the stage is, as it were, the canvas on which the composer expresses his ideas; the choice of the music, scenery and costumes are his colours; the composer is the painter.

Here is the first, clearest and most articulate espousal of the dance-drama, in which music, costumes, dancing and scenery combine to express a single theme or story. It was also a reaction against the superficiality and unreality of the ballets of Noverre's time, so that he could demand "less of the Fairy Tale, less of the marvellous, more truth and more realism". He attacked the ballets of his predecessors for concentrating solely on virtuosity and spectacle, in which "dancing is introduced for the mere sake of dancing".

It is remarkable that Noverre's ideas are, in many ways, so relevant to some of the ballets created in our own time. I believe, in fact, that he was basically mistaken, as we shall see later, but I can imagine no more accurate criticism of the ballets of Balanchine than the following:

> Those figure dances which express nothing, which present no story, which have no character, which do not sketch for one a connected and logical plot, which possess nothing dramatic, and which fall as it were from the skies, are only, in my opinion . . . simple dancing *divertissements* which merely display the limited movements and mechanical difficulties of the art.

The influence of this manifesto had a profound effect on Michel Fokine, as did the art of Isadora Duncan, and it lies behind several of his five principles of the dance. I quote them in full from his letter, since without an understanding of them the development of ballet in our time is, to a large extent, meaningless. Fokine writes:

> Not to form combinations of ready-made and established dance-steps, but to create in each case a new form corresponding to the subject, the most expressive form possible for the representation of the period and the character of the nation represented—that is the first rule of the new ballet.
>
> The second rule is that dancing and mimetic gesture have no meaning in a ballet unless they serve as an expression of its dramatic action, and that they must not be used as a mere *divertissement* or entertainment, having no connection with the scheme of the whole ballet.
>
> The third rule is that the new ballet admits the use of conventional gesture only when it is required by the style of the ballet, and in all other cases endeavours to replace gestures of the hands by mimetic of the whole body. Man can and should be expressive from head to foot.

The fourth rule is the expressiveness of groups and of ensemble dancing. In the older ballet the dancers were ranged in groups only for the purpose of ornament, and the ballet master was not concerned with the expression of any sentiment in groups of characters or in ensemble dances. The new ballet, on the other hand, in developing the principle of expressiveness, advances from the expressiveness of the face to the expressiveness of the whole body, and from the expressiveness of the individual body to the expressiveness of a group of bodies and the expressiveness of the combined dancing of a crowd.

The fifth rule is the alliance of dancing with the other arts. The new ballet, refusing to be the slave either of music or of scenic decoration and recognising the alliance of the arts only on the condition of complete equality, allows perfect freedom both to the scenic artist and the musician. In contradistinction to the older ballet it does not demand "ballet music" of the composer as an accompaniment to dancing; it accepts music of every kind, provided only that it is good and expressive. It does not demand of the scenic artist that he should array the ballerinas in short skirts and pink slippers. It does not impose any specific "ballet" conditions on the composer or decorative artist, but gives complete liberty to their creative powers.

So it was that the concept of the ballet as a unity of its several different components was established, where the dance-drama was seen as its highest manifestation. To this the critics added their chorus of approbation, so that, for book after book, Arnold Haskell carried the message to the faithful: ballet is not just dancing; ballet is a synthesis of music, *décor*, costumes and dance within a single unity. So the public followed. They learned that dancing was not an end in itself, only a means towards the expression of emotion within the framework of a story, of which the greatest examples were provided by Fokine himself—*Petroushka*, *The Firebird* and *Schéhérazade*. He also created *Les Sylphides*, the greatest, most popular and most lasting of all his ballets, which is a little awkward since it does not fit in very readily with his theories. Maybe, one says (once perhaps in a very quiet voice) just because of that; maybe it survives, because it contradicts both Fokine and Noverre, and is "dancing for the mere sake of dancing". It is a nice irony, a curious jest of irreverent time that is no respecter of theories or of persons.

The ballets of Fokine are not, on the whole, the best examples of his theories, and, apart from *Les Sylphides*, they have not survived as significant works for our own time. *Schéhérazade*, once described by a contemporary newspaper critic as "one stupendous orgy", is faded and slightly ridiculous; its famed exoticism now so much fustian, while the opulence of its *décor* by Bakst now reminds one of the decorations to a somewhat dubious massage parlour, run sadly to seed. *The Firebird* was successfully revived by the Royal Ballet, but, apart from a performance by Margot Fonteyn in the title role of exotic and mysterious beauty, it seemed thin in choreography and remote as a legend. *Carnaval* is dead—a quaint piece of Victorian bric-à-brac—and only in the performance of Sally Gilmour as Columbine with the Ballet Rambert did it show any sort of vitality; now the dust has settled on it and can never be blown away again. Even *Petroushka*, despite its powerful symbolism, has little appeal for modern audiences, perhaps because it requires dancers of exceptional personality and dramatic impact in the central roles, for it regained a brief life in the early days of the Festival Ballet when they were played by Massine and Chauviré with a kind of intensity that belongs only to the greatest dancers. But it is a story that wears thin after many repetitions, and it belongs now more to the museum than the theatre. Certain moments, it is true, survive to haunt the imagination: the strange *pas de deux* between the Blackamoor and the Ballerina; the jigging of the puppets in their booth. So, too, one remembers that curious, eerie moment when a young girl is drawn from the crowd towards the Charlatan as he plays his flute, enticed, against her will, by its strange enchantment, and is pulled back by her friends before it is too late, before she also surrenders to his spell. Moments such as this still have power to disturb us, to crowd our minds with dark images, but little else remains of what was once a masterpiece.

But *Les Sylphides* survives, despite so many poor and routine performances, in defiance of time and Fokine's own philosophies. It is, in the main, composed solely of academic steps, thus contradicting the first point of Fokine's manifesto. It has been successfully performed against many different backgrounds and different orchestrations of the music. It has no drama, being an expression of mood only, and so runs counter to his second basic condition. Its use of the *corps de ballet* is, on the whole, entirely traditional; it thus disregards the fourth principle of his manifesto, relating to the use of group movement. Only in the greater freedom given to the dancers in the movement of their arms and upper torso does it show any advance on the academic technique developed by Petipa and Ivanov. Even the costumes are entirely traditional, belonging to the ballets of nineteenth-century Romanticism. As well as this, it is also a masterpiece, a miracle of choreographic invention, whose beauty never palls nor its images lose their resonance and power of evocation.

It is interesting that *Les Sylphides* was created, under the title of *Chopiniana*, in Russia before the advent of Diaghilev's Company to the West, and in this form it survives in the performances of the Kirov Ballet that are danced with so perfect a sense of style, such incomparable musicality and beauty of line, that the ballet is more powerful in this its first design than in any of the subsequent modifications to the choreography made by Fokine himself.

In the performance of Natalia Makarova one is able to appreciate the full beauty of Fokine's invention, for its refinements are beyond the reach of most Western dancers. All the abandoned dreams of the Romantic Age live again in her dancing, so that the ghosts of long ago—Taglioni, Grisi and Grahn—share with her in secret the mysteries of their art. Even in her poses she seems on the brink of flight, held only by those voices that speak to her out of the music and to which she listens, fingers to her lips, as they whisper to her in the silence. Makarova's performance is a miracle of evocation, containing in every pose, every movement of fleeting beauty, the essence of Romantic art. But even without this, *Les Sylphides* remains indestructible, immortal as its chosen spirits who dance beneath the moon.

The only other ballet of Fokine that still has in it the possibility of survival is *Le Spectre de la Rose*, and it is significant that here again it survives in defiance of his own theories. Its weakness is in the choice of music: Weber's *Invitation to the Dance* is pretty, delicate, but basically sentimental, belonging more to the teashop than the theatre, and this acts counter to the remarkable and original dances Fokine created for Nijinsky, where the exotic, almost elemental quality of the movement preserves the memory of that great dancer better than any photograph or memoir of his time. But the dance is too strong, too rich to be carried on so flimsy a score, so that the work is ill-balanced and, in a sense, unmusical. Further, it requires great dancers to interpret it, so that it is strange that Nureyev and Fonteyn did not appear in it some years ago when they were both so magnificently suited to it, as are their opposite numbers in the Soviet Union, Vassiliev and Maximova. The ballet was recently revived at Sadlers Wells by the Royal Ballet, but the central role was so miscast that it made no impact; for some strange reason Anthony Dowell who, it would seem, is ideally suited to the part, was not chosen to dance it.

The ideas of Fokine with their emphasis on the dramatic nature of ballet, expressed in an organic unity of its various components, dominated the work of the first period of the Diaghilev Company. To Western audiences, it was their exoticism, best demonstrated in works like *Le Pavillon d'Armide*, *Cléopâtre*, *Schéhérazade*, the dances from *Prince Igor*, *Thamar* and *Le Coq d'Or*, that made the greatest appeal; to them this was the Russian Ballet, though, in fact, these works were created in opposition to what Fokine considered to be the decadence of the Imperial Theatre. In time, however, the Diaghilev Company began to lose touch with its roots in the traditional Russian ballet; it fell under the influence of Western ideas both in dance and decoration, and began to become a fashionable toy for intellectuals to play with. It seems that Diaghilev recognised the danger, so that his revival of *The Sleeping Beauty* in 1921, for which he imported the two greatest classical ballerinas of the Imperial School, Olga Spessivtzeva and Vera Trefilova, to dance the leading role, can be seen as an attempt to re-establish the classical tradition within his Company. It was a financial disaster, though from it were to stem the revivals of the ballets by Petipa and Ivanov by the Vic-Wells Company a decade later, as a result of which the classical tradition of the dance was fully established in the West.

The final period of the Diaghilev Ballet was a frenzied era where the dance became increasingly modish and chic, at the whim of every change in Parisian fashion, empty and decadent. How far the ballet had declined in this last decade was made ever more apparent in the recent revival of Massine's *Parade* by the Festival Ballet. The effect was staggering; seldom can such a work, with so many distinguished collaborators—Massine, Picasso, Cocteau and Satie—have proved to be so pointless, absurd and trivial as *Parade*, not only pointless, but silly also, a sort of cocktail-party joke of incredible inanity. To this end had the great adventure come. The Company did not cease to exist with Diaghilev's death; it was dead, artistically, long before that, buried under the weight of fashion and second-rate intellectualism.

Yet it seems to me that the seeds of its dissolution were sown in those early, triumphant years; by the abandonment of the classical dance as the central feature of a ballet in favour of choreographic experiment, over-elaboration of *décor* and the choice of unsuitable music for the dance, it destroyed itself, and time took its revenge over the years and at its leisure. One critic alone and one great ballerina, whom he admired with a total dedication, saw the danger; for André Levinson was a critic and not a courtier, and, above all, he cherished the classical dance. He attacked the aesthetics of the Diaghilev Ballet unceasingly, and time has proved him right. He assailed Diaghilev for giving prominence to the painter and the musician over the dancer; he condemned the fake exoticism of many of the ballets; he saw the decadence of the art implicit in its most famous manifestations. Writing in *La Danse d'Aujourd'hui*, he makes his final and crushing indictment:

But they always sought their inspiration outside the dance as such. They always—and this was the initial flaw in their aesthetic— deformed and twisted it, adapted it to express what was foreign to it. It never developed freely, independent of all pastiche and parody, as "a pure act of metamorphosis" as Valéry would have said.

We have already stated our principal objection to the outlook and interpretation of the Ballets Russes at all the successive stages of their triumph and decline. By depriving the dance of its autonomy and incorporating it in a dance-drama which, although ingenious, was ornate, hybrid and lifeless, the directors of this famous company committed it to the whim of the day and destroyed the continuity of a choreographic tradition which is one of the supreme expressions of Western culture.[1]

It is difficult today not to agree that Levinson was right, and that the aesthetics of the Diaghilev Ballet were founded on a huge misconception that the dance was only one of the several components of a ballet. It is, of course, true that the ballets against which Fokine rebelled in the repertoire of the Imperial Theatre were often trivial and foolish, but the classical dance remained in them, however much other aspects were neglected. This Anna Pavlova understood. The works in which she appeared were often of little choreographic worth, but they were transformed by her genius, protected by the care she had for the classical dance, so that it is to her influence, rather than to that of Diaghilev, that the present world of the ballet remains true to its inheritance. When Arnold Haskell writes in *Balletomania* that Pavlova asked him whether he was on her side or on that of Diaghilev, he does not seem to have understood the implication of her statement; what she was asking was whether he stood on the side of the classical dance, or whether he accepted its diminuation, and he had no valid reply to make.

It would, of course, be foolish and ungenerous not to concede that modern ballet is greatly indebted to Diaghilev: he extended the range of the dance enormously, so that it became accepted as a serious art form, to which the greatest composers, designers and painters had a major contribution to make. Further, in the ballets of Massine, *The Three-Cornered Hat*, *La Boutique Fantasque* and *The Good-humoured Ladies*, a new world of movement was discovered with all the richness, humanity and

[1] For French text, see page 173.

detail of the greatest novels. He encouraged new choreographers, including Balanchine, Massine and Lifar, who were to have a profound influence on the future of ballet, and his company became a revolutionary force in the cultural life of his times, causing a profound shift in sensibility that still affects us today. And all this was done without State aid, vast subsidies or any continuous patronage. From his ideas were to emerge the Vic-Wells Ballet and the Ballet Rambert, and the subsequent revival of modern ballet throughout the Western world. It is an amazing achievement, but Levinson's criticism stands. Only in Russia was the great inheritance of the classical dance maintained, even though for many years it was not to develop in any significant way, until the beliefs of Agrippina Vaganova, that were in part derived from those of Fokine, began to bear fruit in the dancers of the Kirov Ballet, who are now the guardians of that tradition and its greatest exponents.

It was to the old Imperial Theatre that Diaghilev had to look when he wished to revive *The Sleeping Beauty*, and this emphasizes the fact that he knew his Company had grown too far from its roots and in too shallow earth. And he was right. It was left to his successor, Ninette de Valois, to restore to the art the primacy of the classical dance. This she did by engaging Sergeyev to mount the classical ballets of Petipa for her young Company, and to build these around a great classical ballerina, Alicia Markova. In her book, *Invitation to the Ballet*, Dame Ninette is quite explicit about her first priority in creating a repertoire: this was to restore traditional classical and romantic works to their rightful place at the centre of the design. This (she wrote) "constitutes the foundation-stone, technical standard and historical knowledge that is demanded as a 'means test' by which the abilities of the young dancers are both developed and inspired." Without these works no true classical ballerina could emerge from within the Company; and she did emerge, and, over thirty years, became as great an influence as Anna Pavlova in establishing the true image of the classical dancer and the nobility and expressiveness of the classical style throughout the Western world. It could certainly be argued that it is a weakness of the English school that Margot Fonteyn has left no true successor, but the standard has been established so uncompromisingly that it cannot be betrayed. Without Fonteyn, we should not have been able to recognise the style when we encountered it again in the dancers of the Kirov Ballet.

It was not surprising that the first company to visit London after the war, Les Ballets des Champs-Elysées, headed by Roland Petit and a number of brilliant soloists, was greeted with delight by the older ballet-goers and critics. Here were the snows of yester-year; here the Diaghilev Company lived again. Many great painters and designers had been asked to decorate the ballets, and the results, in the works of Clavé, Bérard and Wakhevitch, were beautiful and original. Certain ballets of Petit, notably *Le Jeune Homme et La Mort*, *Les Forains* and *Le Rendez-vous* were masterpieces of theatrical invention. There was no *corps de ballet*, only a group of dazzling principals, technically superb and with a style and personality far more dominating than those of their fellow dancers in the Sadlers Wells Ballet.

No one who saw them can forget the excitement of that season, the impact of Jean Babilée (possibly the greatest male dancer to be seen in London since Nijinsky), Nathalie Philippart and Renée Jeanmaire. The company later changed its name, achieved a huge popular success with Petit's *Carmen* and *Le Loup*, and then disintegrated. Petit's talents declined sadly, and he was afterwards to gain the distinction of creating, in *Paradise Lost*, just about the worst and most vulgar spectacle ever to be seen at Covent Garden. The great Jeanmaire became known as "Zizi" to a vast public, later to emerge as the brilliant star of the music hall at the Casino de Paris. The older critics moved away sadly: the snows had melted; it had been no new dawn. And it could not be: the idea of ballet as a composite art form had no real validity. Frederick Ashton's *Symphonic Variations*, performed at Covent Garden in the same month that Les Ballets des Champs-Elysees arrived in London, restored the classical dancer, in a modern work, to her true inheritance. Fokine's manifesto, which he himself denied in his own masterpiece, *Les Sylphides*, was from then on a matter of history, and no longer one of aesthetics.

Ashton's first intention was a ballet of an allegorical nature on the theme of rebirth, but as rehearsals progressed he fined down the work to a purely abstract design, danced by the six most musical artists of the Company. It remains, however, in one sense a ballet of rebirth: the emergence of the dance after the long dark years of the war; the springtime of the earth and of the heart. It is a work true to the history of English lyric verse, and the linked dances are like stanzas of Herrick, Clare or de la Mare, in which the dance is shaped in the same long, flowing lines as the poems. It is the dance seen as song—the natural song of birds set against the movements of the trees on an early summer afternoon and the rippling of the wind. The adoption of Grecian costumes for the girls, together with Ashton's wonderful sense of design, where the dance is framed by dancers posed like statues on each side of the stage, seem far closer to the spirit of the early dances of ancient Greece than any reconstruction of these by Isadora Duncan and her followers. Ardent and innocent, the dancers float over the music as swallows might skim across the wind, free in the luminous air. Here the classical dance is stripped of all its excrescences and distortions that had marked so much of the choreography of the Diaghilev era, and returned to a state of primal innocence, as it might be seen at the dawn of the world. For thirty years its beauty has remained undimmed; at each revival it emerges with all the suddenness and the astonishment of Spring.

From the beginning of his career Ashton had been drawn to the classical dance, free from the encumbrances of plot or dramatic development, and here at last the dance was liberated and restored to its rightful place as the dominating feature of any ballet, no longer the unwilling partner, but the master of a wide uncluttered stage. Earlier, in the exquisite *variation* for the ballerina in *Les Rendezvous*, in which she shapes and freezes the music with a kind of insouciant daring, Ashton had affirmed the primacy of the ballerina and the classical dance, and *Symphonic Variations* was the culmination of these beliefs in one choreographic statement of extraordinary truth and beauty. The ballet had been too long in the thrall of its dark angel, the dance-drama, and, after *Symphonic Variations*, it could never be quite the same again.

This is not to imply that the dance-drama, as established by Fokine, has no longer any validity; for there is room for all types of ballets, but after *Symphonic Variations* one could no longer think of it as being the highest expression of the dance, as Fokine had affirmed. It has not the capacity to survive the years to the same extent as the ballet of pure dance: *Les Sylphides* survives, but all the other ballets of Fokine are little more than museum pieces, essays in make-believe, and lacking, because of that, the ability to speak to different generations in a language that each would understand. At the time of the creation of *Symphonic Variations* it was widely believed that it would not last, and that the future was with the dramatic ballets of Helpmann and de Valois, but the truth was different, and the theorists, by one ballet, were proved to be wrong.

One does not wish to minimise the force of Ninette de Valois' ballets inspired by different painters—*Job* (William Blake), *The Rake's Progress* (Hogarth), *Bar aux Folies Bergères* (Manet), *The Gods Go a-Begging* (Watteau) and *The Prospect Before Us* (Rowlandson)—nor to the superb male dances in the expressionist style she created, those for Mr O'Reilly, Satan and The Man with the Rope, which are masterpieces of plastic imagery and originality of conception, but, after a time, they lose their power to move us, or to stimulate our imagination. For the truly lasting quality of the dance-drama is not due to its narrative or to its characterisation, still less to any real or imagined unity of dance, music and decoration, but to the strength of its imagery—in other words when it is used as a form of emotional expression, where it is equally at home in the abstract ballet or the dance-drama. It is the dance itself, the dance alone, that speaks most clearly to the heart. This is why Anna Pavlova (who was, incidentally, Ashton's first inspiration to become a dancer) reached such huge numbers of people by her art. It did not depend on the originality of the choreography, most of which was academic and fairly banal, nor on her costumes or *décor*, nor even on the music, which was trivial and sentimental; but it was because she allowed her emotions to speak through the language of the dance, which became the expression of her inner nature and the truths of her imagination. The same can be said of Natalia Makarova's dancing in the minute *pas de deux, Spring Waters*, with which I shall deal in more detail when I come to discuss the ballerina. It is in the force of its images, and in the sincerity of the dancer in shaping those images, that ballet achieves its fullest expression; indeed the apologists of the dance-drama can be put to flight by one dancer of genius alone on an empty stage, as Anna Pavlova proved conclusively in *The Dying Swan*.

The dance-drama reached its limits of expressiveness in certain ballets by Antony Tudor, and it is difficult to see how it can be developed further. In *Lilac Garden, Dark Elegies* and, to a lesser extent, in *Pillar of Fire*, Tudor probed deep into the heart of human experience, so that the dance-drama became less a question of narrative and characterisation and more a study of the dark and hidden springs of our unconscious life. The characters were not figures of make-believe, but prototypes of an universal validity with whom audiences could achieve the closest identification, for it was their loss, their grief that they could observe in these ballets, the secrets of their own tired or wounded hearts.

Tudor's works are based on the classical technique, though this is greatly extended and amplified by ideas taken from other schools of the dance, and they have a compression of imagery, an intensity of mood never before achieved in the ballet. He was able, by a single gesture, a single image, to encompass a whole range of human emotion, in the same manner as the acting of Duse (as Shaw noted) was composed of gestures speaking a truth beyond the limit of ordinary words. At the same time Tudor achieved a miraculous flow of movement of unsurpassing beauty, where the dancers were so closely related to one another that every image caused a shift in the total pattern, as if, like a fine web, it trembled at each touch. In many ways *Lilac Garden* achieves the same effect as the great novels of Virginia Woolf that were being published for the first time during the period this and similar ballets were being composed, so that one sensed the movements of unconscious life beneath the images of the dance. As a study of human grief *Dark Elegies* has never been surpassed; it is a statement of such nobility, eloquence and anguished beauty that it remains one of the few great master-pieces of contemporary ballet, huge in its proportions, majestic in its line, universal in its humanity.

In *Undertow* and *Pillar of Fire* Tudor searched deeper into unconscious life, but, as a result, the ballets lost something of the humanity that filled his earlier works with so profound a sense of compassion. *Pillar of Fire* is weakened by a poor and sentimental ending, while *Undertow* partakes more of the nature of a psychiatrist's case-book than a study of recognisable human emotion. In later works, notably *Shadowplay* and *Knight Errant*, composed for the Royal Ballet, Tudor has shown that he is by no means a spent force in contemporary ballet, while *Echoing of Trumpets*, although the theme is too painful, too brutal, ever to have a wide appeal, shows all his old ability to transform the classical dance into images of grief and desolation, far beyond the reach of any other choreographer of our time. He is, in a sense, an isolated figure—an artist of genius who, like Nijinsky before him, is likely to leave no true successor, though his influence on contemporary ballet has been a profound one, so that there can scarcely be a single choreographer working today who has not, in some manner, been affected by his work and incorporated his ideas into their own ballets. It is tragic that this great artist has not, since the days with Ballet Rambert in London, been given a stable company to work with and dancers with enough sensibility, technique and power of imagination to incorporate his vision. He remains a solitary genius who has not even been fully recognised in his own country.

It might seem that, in denying the dance-drama the primacy given to it by Noverre and Fokine, one must be forced into accepting the entirely plotless works of Balanchine in return. But this is not so. As we have seen, Balanchine's work is empty, academic and basically unmusical; it has none of the emotional force of the greatest dance-dramas, such as *The Rake's Progress* or *Lilac Garden*, while it is based on an unimaginative and monotonous use of the academic technique that denies it any true expressiveness. His ballets are a dead end, pointing only to the decadence of the classical style. One must look, if considering the future of the dance, to where a fusion is achieved between the emotional expressiveness and humanity of Tudor's ballets and a new statement of the abstract dance, freed from the crude mechanism of plot or dramatic development, since these are not the prerogative of the dance but of the novel and drama.

The content of the dance must arise naturally from its form; as Coleridge puts it in his lectures on Shakespeare, it is necessary to "harmonise the natural and the artificial". The reason for this can best be expressed in his own words, since they apply as much to the ballet as to poetry: "The organic form is innate; it shapes, as it develops, itself from within, and the fullness of its development is one and the same with the perfection of its outward form."

If we consider the greatest works of twentieth-century ballet *Les Sylphides*, *Lilac Garden*, *Dark Elegies*, *Symphonic Variations*, *Dances at a Gathering* and *Voluntaries*—it can, I think, be seen that they all have common elements. The first is profound emotional content; the second is great musicality, where the music is seen as the source of that emotional life. Further, they are firmly based on the classical dance, and on an extension, but not a distortion of that style. They incorporate a wide range of human emotion within a single emotional spectrum, whether it be of grief in *Dark Elegies* and *Lilac Garden*, or the vulnerability of youth in *Dances at a Gathering*, or of yearning, nostalgia and idealised love in *Les Sylphides*; while in both *Symphonic Variations* and *Voluntaries* the dance is a statement of the creative process both in the artist himself and in the whole rhythmic design of nature. They do not depend on costume or decoration, for here the primacy of the dance is totally affirmed. They deal with human relationships, even in an idealised manner like *Les Sylphides*, but relationships expressed not in terms of imaginary characters, but purely in terms of the dance. They are highly dramatic, yet they have no plot: and they are also firmly based on the realities of human experience, so that the dancers greet one another, relate to one another, in a manner that is entirely natural and human.

In them the dancer is treated as a human being, not a puppet, not a series of notes on a score, nor an artifice, someone playing a theatrical role. They preserve the classical dance; they restore to it its humanity; they affirm, above all, the high seriousness of ballet as an art. These ballets are a stage in the development of a great tradition, and it is the young choreographers of our time, notably Glen Tetley and Hans van Manen, who will draw upon that inspiration further to humanise and extend the range of the classical dance.

All these ballets are supremely musical, where the dance is contained but not dominated by the rhythm, and the phrasing and line of the music are made visible, so that the dancer is a kind of echo, in the music of her limbs, of the music itself. The emotional pattern of the ballets shifts and reforms, so that we do not experience it in the movements of any single dancer, but it is related also to the emotional pattern she makes with the other dancers on the stage. In these great works form and content become one: the formal dance expresses the emotional content of the music, is one with it as the singer is one with his song.

One can single out moments of the most intense emotion from these ballets: in *Dark Elegies*, when a dancer pauses and draws with her arms a kind of geometrical pattern in the air, a gesture of sudden repose in such great anguish; the stillness of the dancers, grouped together at the end of *Lilac Garden*, while the music swirls around them, as if their grief had been let loose on the world like one of the elements of nature, and was heard by them in the music as if in the voice of another being; the wonderful ending to a *pas de deux* in *Dances at a Gathering* when the young couple suddenly draw apart, frightened by the enormity of love that has suddenly engulfed their games of innocence and daring, or when the male dancer leans down to touch the earth with his hand in a perfect image of Blake's words: "all that lives is holy", summarising the very essence of the ballet's philosophy. One remembers, too, at the huge organ chord that opens *Voluntaries*, how the two dancers who have been moving until then in silence, spring to life, jubilant and triumphant, like two stars that blaze suddenly in an empty sky.

So also one recalls the ballerina carried by her partner across the stage in *Symphonic Variations*, floating as if the music were the air she treads with such impalpable lightness. But perhaps of all memories remains the whole of the Prelude in *Les Sylphides*, the most perfect evocation of music ever achieved in the classical dance.

When we hear music we envisage it in our unconscious as it might be if expressed in visible form, not in a picture drawn from life or nature, which is the case with "programme music", but a pattern of curves and changing lines, vibrant with emotion that contains each design and is expressed by it, so that these invisible shapes in our mind are a kind of emotional language beyond the reach of words or reason. This is perfectly achieved in the Prelude, where the dancer shapes every curve and echo in the singing line of her whole body, so that the music is taken up and infinitely extended by her limbs and the line of her arms, that shift to every current of melody as if they rested upon it, drifted on these magical tides. It is the supreme test of a dancer, and in the innumerable performances I have seen there have been only two—those of Tatiana Riabouchinska and Margaret Barbieri—that caught every nuance of the music, so that they could let it shape their movements with an exquisite finality.

The art of choreography is self-renewing, for it draws its images both from the outer world and the secret world of an artist's imagination, where each unite in the dancer, set equidistant between them both. Most ballets are ephemeral, beautiful and fleeting as their dancers, but the few I have mentioned survive and are continually renewed by new generations of dancers, the inheritance of their art. On rare and memorable occasions a new ballet will take up its place as part of this great lineage, as did Hans van Manen's *Four Schumann Pieces*, first danced by the Royal Ballet in January 1975.

It is a work of such exquisite musicianship and rare imagination that it can at once be accepted as a masterpiece both for our time and for the future. The manner in which each musical phrase is carried through the dance, shaping itself with such finality in the curve of arm or leg, where it grows organically from one movement to another, even to its most tiny echo, is a miracle of creative art. Every detail of the score finds its exact equivalent in the dance which, mirror-like, reflects each nuance, each trembling line. Indeed the music is passed from one performer to another almost as if it were itself another dancer, moving between them, linking them together like the lines of a song. The dancers find a new language for each episode in the music, sometimes in images heart-rending in their simplicity, at others in patterns as intricate and brilliant as the shimmer of reflected stars.

In its clarity, the density and compression of its language, in the perilous beauty of its floating lifts, where the dancers are carried like blossoms on the wind, this great work extends and ennobles the classical dance both as an expression of formal design and of emotional truth. Superbly performed by the three finest and most musical artists in the Company—Anthony Dowell, Jennifer Penney and Lesley Collier—*Four Schumann Pieces* contained all the beauty and poignancy of the Spring, expressed by three artists in the springtime of their art. The balance within the music between lyricism and brilliant design was matched by the dancers van Manen had chosen—Jennifer Penny, in the wistful poetry of whose dancing are seen the shadows of twilight, in Lesley Collier the heat and dazzle of high noon. In its warmth, humanity and the singleness of its vision, *Four Schumann Pieces* creates a world of absolute beauty as pure and flawless as a single rose, a world indeed beyond the reach of any other formal art.

These ballets are masterpieces because they include a multiplicity of images, expressive of many emotional states, caught up and framed in music. They contain the best of the dance-drama, the power of images, with the highest in the abstract dance, the poetic statement of emotion as seen through music. In the interrelationship between the dancers and the shifting pattern of emotion they express the ebb and flow of thought itself. So they belong equally to the movement of our blood, the beating of our hearts, even to the great rhythms that enclose all created nature. It is the world of the spirit and the flesh, set within a formal design. They are, indeed, an image of human life, in all its sad brevity and all its brave endeavours.

Attitude derrière ouvert

Arabesque croisé à tenu

Relevé devant ouvert

Attitude devant en fondu

Penché arabesque

Attitude devant en fondu

4th position *croisé*

4th position *croisé*

13. The Dancer: Then

With most dancers the choreography is something outside themselves which they interpret with the maximum fidelity to encompass the choreographer's vision, but with the greatest of dancers there is this, yet there is more than this; their dancing is the expression of their deepest nature within a formal design, an art that goes beyond interpretation to become a personal statement of their most profound beliefs. They do not interpret love or grief; they express their own loving, their own grieving, in a manner that transcends the limitations of the classical form. They are concerned with an inner truth, hidden in the music and within the choreographic design that music encloses, and it is their own discovery, the adventure of their own being expressed in the dance.

The performer and her role are not two separate entities; they merge and coalesce into one. What the choreographer designs for her is only the basic, formal structure; this she absorbs within herself, so that it is expressed as a personal vision that she has discovered within the secrecy of her own heart. At this level of expression, the actual quality or originality of the steps she performs matter little: to watch a ballerina hold an *arabesque*, poised and on the brink of flight, or to see her run across the stage, gives one a greater insight into the nature of the dance than one could find in the most intricate and beautiful choreography that is performed as it were from the outside and not as an expression of the ballerina's inner nature. It is impossible to say how this is done: it is something to do with the

E

phrasing of the dance within the musical structure, something that concerns timing, stress and emphasis, but it will always, finally, remain a mystery.

To write of the ballerina is to be confronted by the mystery of genius and of art. It is the same mystery that one encounters in poetry: how it is that a few simple words, written in a certain order, have the power to move one, yet the most elaborate verbal structure will leave one indifferent. Here is one example:

> The moving moon went up the sky
> And nowhere did abide,
> Softly she was going up
> And a star or two beside.

It is the same with a great ballerina. When she raises her arms, it is as if she reaches to draw the moon down, or touch with her fingers the most distant star; yet what is this, in dance terms, but one of the five positions of the arms, no different, on the surface, from the same gesture made by all those dancers we have now forgotten? To try and dissect it is futile; one might just as well pluck the petals from a rose in an attempt to discover the secret of its beauty. All that one can say is that her dancing is one with all that grows and moves and is reborn; it is one with the great winds of summer that fan beneath the trees, one with the slow unfolding of the petals of a rose, one with the eternal beating of the sea, the movement of a turning tide. It is the dance of all created things.

The continuity of a great tradition in ballet is indeed more clearly seen in its ballerinas than in any other performer or choreographer. For many decades this was handed on from one to another, since no adequate method of dance notation had been evolved, and, even today, the two main systems of notation cannot be expected to give every shade or nuance of an interpretation. In a sense, therefore, the young dancer at the *barre* is surrounded by ghosts, by the movement of long-stilled limbs, the haunting of vanished smiles. Her inheritance is a proud one; it reaches back into the nineteenth century, where those frail phantoms of the Romantic Ballet drifted through their enchanted woods and the palaces and gardens of a legendary art.

It is an inheritance that has often been betrayed, not by the dancers themselves, but by certain choreographers and *maîtres de ballet*, so that the ballerina has been forced to appear in roles that deny by every movement her tradition.

In this and the final chapter, I wish to consider a group of great ballerinas, four of the past and five of the present, who might be considered the supreme exemplars of the classical dance. For those of the past, I shall draw mainly on the writings of André Levinson who has recorded immortally the styles of many performers at the beginning of the century, in the same manner as did Théophile Gautier of the dancers of his time. To read Levinson's description of the dancing of Pavlova, Spessivtzeva and Trefilova is as close as we can ever be to the mysteries of their art; in the exquisite balance of his prose, as classical and beautifully formed as the limbs of these dancers, he makes us see them dance again, and beneath his lines we hear the long-forgotten music play, and see the curtain rise on a distant stage.

Even if one has not read his criticism, one can still see the shadow of these famous names, as it lies around each dancer today, even though she may be unaware of her inheritance. For example, after the interpretations of Pavlova, Karsavina and Spessivtzeva, the character of Giselle took on a new depth, a new force, a new resonance that has now become part of the traditions of the role. So also, among its greatest exponents, some have been coached by their illustrious predecessors: Ulanova has, for many years, helped Ekaterina Maximova with the role, and, more recently, Yvette Chauviré has advised Eva Evdokimova, so that the tradition has been preserved for a new generation of dancers and audiences. In the same manner, after the performances of Natalia Makarova in *Swan Lake*, no ballerina is expected to give the superficial reading of the main role that was customary some years ago; it has found another dimension, a new richness in its symbolism of which probably its first interpreters were wholly unaware. The ballerinas I write about in this chapter cannot therefore ever be forgotten; they live on in today's dancers, and because of this they have defied time and all its cruel ambiguities.

Vera Trefilova

Maybe it has been lost to us for ever, the old Imperial style of the Russian Ballet; or maybe it has been transformed by all the great dancers who have guarded it as their inheritance, so that we can never return to it as we can never return to the dancing of Vera Trefilova. Thirty years have passed since the death of one who was, perhaps, the supreme exponent of that style. It belonged to a different type of society from our own; it was grander, more regal, more totally assured than the dancing of our time. Its essence was sculptural, its architecture composed of great sweeping lines and huge perspectives, remote and self-contained in all its lonely splendour, behind which the ballerina guarded the mysteries of her art.

I think it would seem cold to us now, remote and unfeeling; between us and the ballerina today has grown a new relationship, fostered by artists of a rare humanity, such as Karsavina, Pavlova and Fonteyn, that is closer, more personal, even one might say, more loving than what was known before. To be *prima ballerina assoluta* of the Imperial Theatre was to be one set apart, infinitely distant from her audience, empress of the wide stage which was her kingdom. We should admire Trefilova if she danced for us today, revere her even, but I do not think we should love her; indeed I do not think we should dare to be so familiar, or so bold.

Trefilova graduated from the Imperial school in 1894 and became *prima ballerina* in 1906, so that in a way she marks the transition between the old ballet and the new, the last great ballerina in a tradition that was to be challenged by a new society in Russia and by a revolution in the dance abroad. In 1921 she appeared in Diaghilev's production of *The Sleeping Beauty* when she shared the role of Aurora with Olga Spessivtzeva, the other flawless ballerina of her time.

Trefilova's life was a strange and, in some ways, a tragic one. After the death of her second husband (who had pressed her to give up ballet), she retired into a convent as a novice, to emerge later and marry the famous ballet critic, Valerian Svetlov. She then resumed her career, after two incredible years of work to recover her technique, and appeared again on the stage in 1916.

Writing of her, Svetlov says: "What she achieved was little short of a miracle—the combining of individual creation with technical perfection. Her art was free from all artifice, all exaggeration. It was filled with a grace which charmed by reason of its natural nobility and its delicate sense of proportion."

After her retirement she set up her own school in Paris where she could pass on this famous tradition, recalling the days of her glory at the Maryinsky Theatre. She died in 1943, but she has her memorial, like so many other great dancers of the past, in the writings of André Levinson. This is what he had to say of her after her farewell performance in Paris:

> . . . there are many dancers, even mediocre ones, who manage to overcome some difficulty by sheer strength of will or succeed in keeping a brilliant beat by mere chance. But what will always elude them is the perfect cohesion of *enchaînements*, that flow of movement which allows no breaks and which makes of one step by Trefilova what Wagner calls in music the unbroken melody.
>
> In the *adagios*, the play of curves and verticals is of unparalleled beauty; her *développé* is like the opening of a corolla. And her arm movements appear, such is her elegant precision of line, to have been traced by the pencil of Ingres, from the radiant glance down to the tapering *points*. Not for her the dizzy flights or the effusive dances of great passion. Pavlova is the bird; she is the flower. An admirable instrument as well as the composer: a dancing Stradivarius.
>
> No sudden step interrupts this *cantilena* line, no hesitation breaks the flow; and it is this wonderful *legato* which makes of Trefilova's art an articulate language of dance forms. For with her, we are far from these interrupted exclamations or from this intermittent hiccough which, being false in terms of the dance, ends by misleading a section of the public.[1]

Of the dancers of the immediate past, I think that Yvette Chauviré and Nina Vyroubova (who was a pupil of Trefilova) must most closely have mirrored aspects of her style. So, too, Galina Ulanova, although her dancing was seriously marred by Bolshoi-type mannerisms, had that enormous sweep of movement, the authority that belongs to the true *ballerina assoluta* of

[1] For French text, see page 174.

the Imperial school. Of present ballerinas, Natalia Makarova and Eva Evdokimova, in the huge, sculptural architecture of their dancing in the Second Act of *Swan Lake*, must also remind older ballet-goers of their great forerunner.

Trefilova was not suited to emotional roles; she never played Giselle, since that was beyond her scope, and I think there must have been a curious kind of objectivity about her dancing, such as a sculptor might have in relationship to his material. For her what was important was the shaping of the phrase, the whole harmonious balance of her dancing, its majestic design. It is the art of logic with a type of mathematical beauty, where the delight given was due to the sublime proportion of its form.

It does not seem for her to have been a private search for the perfect line that marked the dancing of Olga Spessivtzeva, whose art was a private mediation between herself and the music; rather it was bold and outward, it was designed to please like a great building set within the wide perspective the music afforded her. Like the Fugues of Bach it sought to express no truth beyond the ordering of perfect form, and perhaps indeed this is the highest aim of any art and the most noble achievement of the classical dance.

The end of Trefilova's life—her studio closed, herself impoverished, sick and with few friends—was a tragic one. As Lifar writes with his usual eloquence: "bird of dead ashes, at the end, and no longer bird of fire". So she died, and as a genius of the dance she will always be remembered.

Tamara Karsavina

If Vera Trefilova was the last great ballerina of the Imperial Theatre, Tamara Karsavina was no less surely the first of the modern dance, a link between the two ages. It was she who brought the new Romanticism to Western art, and was its first modern ballerina. The Romantic ideal she embodied was not that of the nineteenth century, which was carried over in the dancing of Olga Spessivtzeva; it was warm and vital and passionate, more truly human, more an expression of her own times; she was not a dream, not the ghost of the imagination, she was the real and loved. Her beauty was serene and untroubled, yet full of mystery; in her great, haunted eyes lay a world of high romance.

The lyrical sweetness of her dancing, her gaiety, her mystery and her noble repose, were of the same world as *The Faerie Queene* and *The Romance of the Rose*, whose chaste beauty has, like her dancing, something of the innocence, the freedom that belong to the first light of the world. In the wide radiance of her candid eyes was seen also the dawn of a new era in theatrical art. As Lifar says very beautifully: "She was of *this* world and she was simple, but her simplicity had in it something of the marvellous."

Karsavina's dancing incorporated a perfect balance between instinct and intelligence, between the creative spirit and the shaping will. Each role she performed was the achievement of constant study and a complete intellectual grasp of its nature; nothing was left to chance, to a moment's inspiration; her art was guided by an intelligence that was always the curb on her imagination. Her exquisitely proportioned body was a gift of nature that has, perhaps, never been so lavishly granted to any other ballerina of her time or our own. In itself, it was a work of art. As Osbert Sitwell writes, "The very pose of her lily-like neck was unforgettable, and there was about her shape and movements a perfection of grace that for the first time made me realise how near are the Russians . . . to the ancient Greeks."

More than that, Karsavina also achieved the reconciliation between the classical dance of the Imperial Theatre and the new choreography of Michel Fokine, but she never lost touch with the springs of her art. Although she appeared for many seasons with the Diaghilev Ballet, she returned often to the Maryinsky where she would dance again in the great ballets of Petipa. She was thus both a classical ballerina within the great tradition and also a modern dancer of a new, astonishing kind. She belonged both to the past and the present, and such was the timeless perfection of her art, that each could claim her as their own. As Arnold Haskell says in his early study of the ballerina: "It was only when Diaghilev, Fokine and Karsavina met that the new ballet was ready to be born out of the old." Yet in her dancing

135

the old classical ballet continued to live on with the new, and between them there was no contradiction.

If one were to compare Karsavina's dancing with its sister art of poetry, one might equate it with the early romanticism of Wordsworth, just as Spessivtzeva represented the later, morbid imagination of poets like Beddoes and Poe, and Pavlova, by her transcending fire, most closely relates to the visionary world of William Blake. These three immortal ballerinas expressed, therefore, different aspects of Romanticism in art in a manner that is unlikely ever to be achieved again in the formal dance.

In her dancing there was also a kind of veiled melancholy; it was the dance of memory and regret, enclosed in a kind of nostalgia that is so typical of Russian art. This would be lightened at moments by a sudden smile, as if the music as it passed her touched her lips briefly like an unexpected kiss. This quality was superbly caught by Fokine in *Le Spectre de la Rose* where nostalgia, yearning and sweet memory combined in her dancing; it had in it all the ardour, all the brief sadness of youth: the vision she saw was not the dancing of a rose, but the passing of all that was beautiful in this transitory world. Left alone, her eyes seeking in vain the moonlit darkness, luminous herself like a pale rose, radiant in its own light, she created an image of youth and the griefs of youth that can never have been surpassed in theatrical art.

Karsavina was more fortunate than her other great contemporaries. Her father was a dancer, a friend of Marius Petipa and later a *maître de ballet*, while her mother was an aristocrat and a woman of considerable culture. She was, therefore, brought up in an atmosphere that developed her high intelligence, so that she was able to achieve in her roles an intellectual distinction that was not granted to other ballerinas. She was in touch, also, with all the cultural ideas of her time. As Lifar says: "She identified herself with her age and was its perfect expression."

Neither Trefilova, Pavlova nor Spessivtzeva had so fortunate a youth; each of them was almost certainly illegitimate, and each was brought up in poverty and mean circumstances. The dance was, for them, the central experience of their artistic lives; for Karsavina, educated with much wider horizons, the dance could be seen as part of the whole cultural background of her time; her attitude was more balanced, serene and harmonious than theirs could ever be. Lifar describes Pavlova and Spessivtzeva, rather unkindly but with some truth, as "dedicated monsters"; for Karsavina he has no hard words to say, noting only her sincerity and the integrity of her artistic ideals.

Perhaps the most beautiful and exact description of her art comes from André Levinson, that supreme chronicler of theatrical genius. He writes:

The sweetness of her physical charms, her likeness to the byronic heroine of some old keepsake, are well matched by the subtlety of her cultivated intelligence. The other great Russian ballerinas are wonderful instinctive dancers. The spirit of the school of the dance, the law of aesthetics which rules it, are glimpsed through their intuitiveness. Karsavina's art is one of conscious effort. She recognises the elements which the school provides and uses them according to her judgment. In this way she achieves a composite and delicate art.

Ghost or sprite, lost soul or dragonfly, Karsavina never loses her exquisite femininity, be she grief-stricken or smiling. She endowed most of Fokine's creations with this feminine essence; she devoted herself to the thinking of this master, to the detriment even of her own technique and, by the quality of her nature, conferred a rare nobility on those of his characters who came close to vulgarity.[1]

So this beloved dancer passes into history and legend. She must always remain the ideal for the young dancer to pursue, since she showed that perfect balance between intelligence and imagination for which the artist seeks, and for which most seek in vain. If truth, integrity and high seriousness are still the aims of every artist, he can take strength from the fact that these were once encompassed in a dancer of genius, whose dancing affirmed the greatness of the ballet as a theatrical art.

Anna Pavlova

She was called by André Levinson "the sublime vagabond" who found no resting place in her travels round the world, but

[1] For French text, see page 174.

rests secure now in memory, this dancer of genius whom the world will never forget. If the dance could be seen in its essential form within any human being, it was in Anna Pavlova, for she and the dance were one, caught up in a single creative act, transfigured into the poses of an immortal art. Made from so little—fragments of old ballets, solos as brief as they were, for the most part, undistinguished—her art shaped from them those sublime images of love and grief that were the truths of her imagination and her inner life.

The dance was an expression of her own being, the distillation of a personality as complex and multicoloured as the arc of a rainbow. Her art was both highly personal and, at the same time, it belonged to all, so that those who watched her shared with her their unknown lives. This was no artifice, no illusion; this was the language of their most secret hearts. In Balzac's words, with Anna Pavlova the dance became a manner of being; it was the only way she could reach into her own strange and troubled nature, and then at so deep a level that the dance became an expression of truths common to all humanity, but secret from them, hidden even in their dreams. She had the universality of genius, found among certain poets and composers, but never before in a dancer.

The singularity of Pavlova may perhaps be found in her sad, impoverished childhood, where she was cossetted and pampered by her grandmother in a way that was to make her the most self-centred of dancers, even though she was often the kindest and most generous of friends. She could never fit within an ensemble, nor dance in the company of artists of a similar standard to herself; and this was nothing so simple as jealousy or small vanities (though she had these in full measure) but because she realised she was unique and that what she had to give she could only give alone. It is significant that her greatest dance was *The Dying Swan*, composed for her by Fokine as a solo to which she alone could bring meaning and the most profound truth. And she gave more than her art; she gave herself to her audiences, showed them the most secret places in her heart, with an unparalleled generosity and a total dedication. Of course, like all pampered children, she wished to be loved, but unlike them, she wished to be loved because of the magnitude of her giving. She had a profound sense of dedication: her art was a mission to the poor and impoverished of spirit, whom she could console and heal through sharing with them the common language of their own humanity.

Anna Pavlova did not need great choreography or great music, for with her the dry academic steps from old forgotten ballets suddenly throbbed with life, became full of hidden resonances. In the same manner as another visionary, William Blake, she needed only simple images with which to express the most profound truth, a truth not acquired by study or conscious application, but known by instinct, by the light of nature, in a single intuitive statement. She worked phenomenally hard to perfect her technique, yet this was only a means towards the expression of her personality that shone through it like the sun through clouds. Her art had that same iridescence that lit up from within every movement of the formal dance, so that it was like a veil of light that hid her from the common glare of the cold, academic technique. It mattered little that her dances were often banal and sentimental, no more than the words matter to a great singer as she floats them on the air.

If there is one feature above all that distinguishes Anna Pavlova, it was her sincerity, in life as in art, between which she saw no divide. Her art was herself, the source and expression of her being. It drew its life from the simple images of nature, and these she transformed into the form of symbolic truths, an allegory of her own inner life. As a woman she could be maddening—spoilt, wilful, intemperate—just because she was so totally spontaneous. If she felt sad, she wept; if she failed to get her way, she indulged in a fit of tantrums; when she knew she was wrong, impulsively she asked for forgiveness. There was in her character no deceit, nothing that was false or distorted; her emotional life was so rich, so varied, that it baffled her friends by its many contradictions. But it was this that she disciplined in the form of the classical dance, so that she was able to pour into it a spirit of astonishing richness and complexity, a nature so prodigal that it never reached the end of its resources.

It seemed that Anna Pavlova reduced to nothing all the

elaborate theories about the art of ballet: she needed only a stage, an audience with whom she could communicate as in a private dialogue with each of them, a small range of academic steps and gestures. That was enough. The poet, after all, also needs only a few words. And Pavlova's dancing had the compression, the ambiguity, the concern for essential images only, that is common to the greatest poetry. Her art was the ordering of truth within a formal design, and in this she was one with the poet also.

It was probably not realised until the time of Anna Pavlova that the classical dance had at its disposal such a huge range of imagery. After all, Fokine had found the ballets of his youth trivial, vulgar and inadequate, and he was right. What he could not have anticipated was what a woman of genius could find within them, having no need for scenery, fine music or even expressive choreography. Pavlova, in fact, restored the primacy of the classical dance to the world of ballet. Because of her we now know that the style is not empty or unreal (as its opponents have so often and so foolishly affirmed); its limits are still beyond our imagination. The fashionable audiences that applauded the ballets of Diaghilev's last period were less wise than those who were totally ignorant of the art, to whom Pavlova danced far from the great opera houses of the world.

André Levinson, an opponent of what Diaghilev and his entourage proclaimed as the new art, was never deceived; he recognised Anna Pavlova as the dancer who had preserved her inheritance, enriched it far beyond the dreams of the choreographers of long ago. In 1929 he writes this, one of his many tributes to her genius:

The "Pavlova phenomenon" is the result of the providential encounter between an individual style and the elements of a formal style, between a prodigiously lively sensibility and an ensemble of formal movements elaborated and selected down the centuries. Pavlova brings a tradition back to life and enriches it . . . The notion of what is permanent, unalterable and universally valued which is contained in our own conception of beauty—the algebra of proportions, the laws of balance and gradation—is spontaneously shown in every movement, turn or leap of this young woman as she dances on *points* in the theatre. For each one of her gestures is seen to be the perfect expression, the most eloquent outward sign of our innermost selves. Her whole being expresses in the most personal way things which are universal, belonging to our time and yet also to all time.

Her dancing reconciles obscure instinct with lucid thought. It is molten liquid being cast into a mould to form a statue. Pavlova possesses the double gift of pouring every emotion into a line of the dance and then of saturating every line with emotion. She is the most passionate of dancers and the most graceful of mimes. The exquisite exuberance of her whole being, the gaiety and anguish overflowing from every movement in a rigorously abstract art explain the fascination wielded by this remarkable Russian star. Pavlova dancing a classical variation is like a flame seen through panes of glass.[1]

In this way, though she has no need of critics or historians, Anna Pavlova was remembered. She belongs to her age and to all ages; neither time nor changing fashion can take from her anything that was her own: she, perhaps of all dancers, is alone and unique in human memory, she the immortal one.

Olga Spessivtzeva

Olga Spessivtzeva, that restless, unquiet spirit, how hard it is to enclose her in a phrase, to secure her in her flight. She came and went so swiftly, out of the shadows of the past, into the cold twilight of a mental collapse, whose darkness then engulfed her for over twenty years. Yet many have affirmed that she was the greatest classical ballerina of her age, with a purity of style, an eloquence of movement, that had never been surpassed. Lifar, who describes himself with more beauty than truth as "almost the only survivor from that kingdom of vanished shades", maintains that she was incomparable, the Muse of the dance; while Anton Dolin, another of her partners, has remained spellbound by her art, its icy perfection, airy and insubstantial like a moonlit ghost. Levinson was perplexed. He called her "morbid" and "a convalescent". She was a dark mystery to him, an inhabitant of an unknown land.

[1] For French text see page 174.

Spessivtzeva seemed like a revenant from the lost ballets of a hundred years ago, whose secret she alone could fully understand, so that she became the greatest Giselle of her own or any other time. She could evoke in her movements a world of dark romance, through which she glimmered, pale and evanescent; her dancing was like the shadow of the music as it passed across the stage. She was the ghost of a vanished age, creature of the night, the bringer of dreams. An atmosphere of mystery clung to her; it seemed to haunt her moon-dazed eyes that turned their gaze so secretly within.

It is apparent that she had not the vividness, the dazzling intensity of Anna Pavlova, nor had she the marbled grandeur of Trefilova, nor the emotional range of Tamara Karsavina. Instead she possessed a kind of poetry, a wistful lyricism that were entirely her own. Indolent and languorous, she seemed in *Giselle* to drift listlessly over the surface of the music, imprinting her feet soundlessly on the air. She was a magical creature, come from another world than our own, who had made the skies her airy habitation, the dark wood of *Giselle* her tomb. No dancer ever had such mystery, nor shaped with her limbs such poses of haunted calm. The night was in her eyes, and its darkness was to become her own.

Spessivtzeva appeared on the stages of Western Europe for less than fifteen years, many of which were spent at the Paris Opéra where she had no opportunity to extend her art. Born in 1895, she trained at the Maryinsky School, and first appeared in the West as Princess Aurora in Diaghilev's magnificent production of *The Sleeping Beauty* at the Alhambra in 1921. The perfection of her style, its purity of line and miraculous extensions, had the quality of song; it brought to the central role a sense of romance that irradiates Tchaikovsky's music.

But it was for her interpretation of Giselle that Spessivtzeva will be remembered. The role suited her temperament exactly, and she distilled within it all the griefs, the loneliness and the hidden fears of her tormented spirit. Her performance spoke directly from her troubled heart. She was able to capture in the First Act the fearful, doom-haunted nature of Giselle, whose joy she knew to be so fleeting and who carried within her the seeds of oncoming madness. Spessivtzeva was herself often alone with her unreasoning fears; this solitude of the young, bewildered girl was her own also, and the tears she wept on the stage were the tears for her own life, her own anguished heart. Like Giselle, for Olga Spessivtzeva the dance in all its sad fragility was not strong enough to contain her tormented spirit.

In the Second Act she achieved the perfect reconciliation, where the spirit of the dead Giselle was still an echo of the betrayed girl. As she rose from the tomb she brought with her the chill of the abandoned grave, the darkness of the cold earth. There was in her dancing a terrible sense of mortality, the loneliness of the soul in the huge void between two worlds. The air was dark, and dark the overshadowing sky where alone she must make her dwelling, this restless spirit of a betrayed love. In her performance it was not the dance itself, but, as it were, the dance reflected in the still waters of the music, where it shimmered in the light, glowed in its own iridescence. It was the dance made so impalpable that it was like a distant reflection of the dancer. Her movements seemed to be shaped by the night winds, her arms to rest, tendril-like, on the surface of the music. This performance was the crown of her artistic life, the justification for all her sad endeavours. I quote Levinson again:

Hers is a being singular and unique, so close to a certain type of choreographic beauty created by Taglioni. Even the long, quivering lines of Spessivtzeva, the ethereal appearance of her whole body, heighten if possible the resemblance to a seraphic Sylphide. The delicacy, the touching fragility of the new Giselle seem almost to derive from frail health. But "la morbidezza" is, in this elegiac dancer, an added attraction. The outlines of the leg movements, the arch of the foot are admirable. A simple *préparation à la quatrième* becomes, with such legs, the expression of a rare beauty.

The body of Spessivtzeva would have been a worthy dwelling place for genius. It was inhabited instead by a strange spirit of sorrow and languor, a resigned and sometimes almost absent soul. Nothing here of that hurricane of the soul which blew over Pavlova. The latter is like a lily gleaming in its artlessness. But Spessivtzeva with her dreamy, ravaged beauty, her bowed head, her gently sloping shoulders, is she not rather the willow tree dear to the twenty melancholy years of Musset?

But this gentle convalescent is a dancer of the greatest span and one of uncommon intelligence. Her long, tapering legs move with splendid reach and freedom. They act as springs in *temps sautés*, lifting her to incredible heights. The fine point of the foot easily supports the body in *relevés* which provoke bursts of applause. And the pose in *arabesque penchée* of this star quivers on a long-held note like the string of an Amati . . . This woman is—if one may modify a famous phrase—a dancing reed.[1]

Olga Spessivtzeva's mind grew more deeply troubled and finally collapsed into insanity. For over twenty years she remained in a mental home. Then suddenly she began to recover: the terrible shadows lifted, and she was free at last and at peace. Her life had been more tragic than that of any of the doomed heroines she portrayed on the stage with such consummate art. She had tried, with a terrible intensity, to find within the logic of the classical dance a world of reason, a quest in movement for inner peace; and it was this that gave to her dancing its curious isolation, marked, too, the intensity of her fear She paid a terrible price in human suffering, yet without this her genius might never have been expressed, and the portrait of Giselle, that miraculous night flower of art, might never have blossomed in the haunted wood.

[1] For French text, see page 175.

14. The Dancer: Now

A young ballerina today is the inheritor of all the ages of the classical dance; in her they find their fulfilment, their brief resting place. This is the glory of the classical ballet, and for this reason the ballerina takes the stage so proudly, knowing that it is her ineluctable right, the bequest she owns. So the dance is continually renewed; the past and the present meet in a single gesture, and are by this wholly reconciled.

The dancers of the past, whom we have just glimpsed, left after them this immense legacy. They can never be forgotten, for the dance is continuous. We may not have seen them, yet we see them every night we go to the ballet. For the stage is peopled by ghosts, these dancers from long ago, assured of their survival, serene and untroubled by the deceits of time.

I want now to paint in outline portraits of dancers of our own time, knowing that they are representative of so many more I have not space to mention. They are the inheritors of this unbroken tradition which is theirs to enrich and to hand on to their successors. One of these great ballerinas, Dame Margot Fonteyn, is near the end of her career, so that we can look down the long gallery of portraits she has created, now lit by the evening sun; for another, Eva Evdokimova, despite her wide and varied experience, it is still high summer, and the greatest may yet to be. Yet, in a sense, all of them exist out of time, for the art they represent belongs also to what Lifar described as "that kingdom of vanished shades". The tradition is maintained: what for one is the twilight will, for another, be the dawn. The classical dance is thus new-made in each new dancer, is restored in all its splendour as each for the first time takes the stage.

Margot Fonteyn

She is the bringer of a great calm, the wide tranquillity of a summer's art, cool in the after-glow of noon. The radiance of Fonteyn's dancing is now beginning to fade, to become lost in our memories of her, yet all who watched her during this stupendous career from the Vic-Wells Ballet to the flowering of her art at Covent Garden in the years following the war will never watch ballet in quite the same way again. She brought to it a new kind of poetry and a new humanity, raised the classical dance from a study of form to a personal encounter with her audience, a shared experience of the music and the emotion that lay hidden within it.

Although much has changed now, much diminished, the real core of her dancing remains unaltered; it is essentially musical and does not depend to any large extent upon a declining technique. Her dancing grows from the still centre of the music, in the same manner as a melody rises out of the silence and shapes its design fastidiously on the air. Each phrase of the dance develops organically from that which preceded it, each with a different tonal colour, blended in slow harmonies and enclosed within her arms. And through the music one feels the radiance of her own personality that lights it from within, as the sunlight illuminates the arch of the sky and becomes one with it, suffuses it with its own brightness.

The sensitivity of her line is such that the music seems to make its own tiny alterations to it, in the angle of arms or head, appearing to adjust this visual harmony to a closer accord with the melodic design. Fonteyn does not so much dance to the music, she allows the music to carry her along, shaping the pattern of her limbs, not only with a supreme logic, but also with a kind of emotional truth that can only be achieved by an artist of rare sincerity and dedication. Her dancing is a slow enchantment, the working of a gradual spell. It does not astonish one, nor make one hold one's breath with excitement;

it leads one very gently, but with complete determination, to the heart of the music where her dance resides. It has a serenity that has been won after arduous endeavour, the stillness of a classic art. That is what I shall most remember about Margot Fonteyn —the sense of repose, where, in quiet order, the miraculous harmonies of the dance are finally resolved. It is an achievement of logic and will, but it is also instinctive, the mystery of her art.

Much has been written about Fonteyn's interpretation of many roles, but less about her own stage personality, both elusive and distinctive, which permeated each one of them. It is a personality at one with her dancing in that it reconciles opposite qualities within a harmonious whole. It has an air of sophistication and also of simplicity; of a quiet, almost ironical sense of humour and a profound seriousness; of intellectual distinction and emotional truth. It is both near us in its warmth, compassion and humanity, yet far away because of a certain detachment from the roles she portrays. It is a conscious art, and an instinctive art; calculated by sheer theatrical skill, yet shaped by an intuitive understanding of the music. It is an art that never draws attention to itself by any feats of virtuosity or deceit; at the same time, it dominates the stage by a kind of personal magnetism that is unique in my experience. In the great classical roles, like Princess Aurora, she was both the *ballerina assoluta* and a young girl, a creature of fantasy and imagination, and a woman in love. In all these balances between two extremes, she achieved the reconciliation within the music, where they were drawn together as two melodies join in the resolution of harmony.

One of the most extraordinary features of her dancing has always been the way she achieves the closest possible relationship between herself and each member of the audience. However large the theatre, she seems to draw them around her, to invite them to join her, so that each performance has a kind of intimacy, whether danced in an opera house or on a tiny stage. Yet it is in no sense a crude invitation, the kind of flattery and false glamour that has destroyed so many fine dancers in the past; it is a question of giving and sharing, allowing them to become involved also in her encounter with the music. I think this is why she has been so greatly loved, with a warmth and sincerity far beyond any other theatrical performer of our times. The public do not like to be tricked or cheated, however much they may roar with applause; they have to be gathered in, through a shared experience of the dance and the music. I have watched Fonteyn hundreds of times from a very considerable distance from the stage, but always she seemed so near me, for she could obliterate space by one glance from her wide and luminous eyes, by one gesture of an exquisite finality and truth. One can never be far away from what is true.

There is also something child-like about her art, a kind of innocence. It has a sense of wonder, of awakening to life, the dawning of love breaking before her delighted eyes. The world into which she invites one is not shadowed, or darkened by strange imaginings, as must have been that of Olga Spessivtzeva; it is lit by a magical light that is the reflection of the music, so that the ballets of Petipa became, in her interpretations, glimpses into some enchanted garden of childhood and pure imagination. They were a kind of fairyland for adults as well as children, a rediscovery of simple truths, those intimations of immortality that are the primal springs of art.

I do not think she ever found within *Swan Lake* or *The Sleeping Beauty* anything extraordinary: with her they became allegories of the human spirit, comprehended by her in no intellectual manner, but by a form of simple acceptance, the belief, when she was on the stage, that this kingdom of once-upon-a-time was real and now. Into the character of Odette she poured all her understanding of human grief, of loneliness and disappointed love; into that of Aurora, her sense of youth and the extreme vulnerability of youth, the first awakening of the heart. They became studies in human nature as she had experienced it, with a kind of intuitive understanding, and they were used to express these discoveries with a quiet assurance and a total sincerity. Her dancing has never been universal, never expressed the greatest flights of the imagination, such as Natalia Makarova was able to achieve in her performances in *The Song of the Earth*; rather, it has been intimate, highly personal and marked by a deep concern for the simple human emotions of love and grief, as they might be known to a child. So she excelled in her portraits of young girls from Giselle to Cloé in *Daphnis and Cloé*; in a glance, one gesture, they revealed the secrets of their hearts—the innocence, the vulnerability and the strength of will that lay so often beneath the fragile surface.

It is true that in her understatement, her quiet wit, Fonteyn showed us a very English art, going back to the plays of Shakespeare and Congreve where the balance between humour and passion is so miraculously achieved, but this was only the surface that concealed huge depths of feeling. One has only to remember the pathos of her mad-scene in *Giselle*, the fierce passion she gave to her role in *Tiresias*, the seductive beauty of her Ondine, to realise the full scope of her gifts. Her art is one of moderation, but never of any shallowness of feeling; it is temperate in the real meaning of the word, the point of exact balance between emotion and will.

Fonteyn is the first great ballerina of the English school, and she may well be the last, in the sense that dancers of later generations have been exposed to a much wider range of styles and teachers than were available to her. For many years she remained sheltered from outside influences, first because in its early days British ballet was a parochial affair, and then the war came to cut her off from foreign dancers, teachers and companies. She was therefore obliged to form herself within this new tradition, created in the main by the choreography of Frederick Ashton, so that when the war ended and the Sadlers Wells Ballet was free to travel abroad again, foreign audiences were amazed to find so original a dancer, so truly herself, so remarkable in her understanding of the limitations of her style. For it has always had limitations, in the same way as lyrical poetry can never achieve the sweep or the majesty of the blank verse line; yet it was, like the songs of Herrick or Campion, a kind of perfect miniature: its poetry was unique—pure, unforced, with a singing line of astounding beauty.

When the Company first visited the United States, Fonteyn's dancing came like a revelation; it was a new discovery in the classical dance—a kind of sublime interlude in a long tradition. Fonteyn then rose to be the greatest figure of international ballet; her dancing became grander, more eloquent, closer indeed to the style of the Imperial Theatre which we were to see, for the first time since the war, in its full splendour with the Kirov Ballet. Maybe indeed she became a greater ballerina, as she absorbed new influences and moved, as a guest artist, among many different companies; but, for me, at least, something was lost: the lyricism of her dancing became overlaid by outside influences; the veiled and haunted poetry of her art, so full of mystery and hidden resonances, diminished, so that now only glimpses of it remain. What she had lost was irretrievable and entirely her own, and we may never experience it again.

I do not watch Margot Fonteyn dancing now; it spoils my memories of her, but, in a sense, her dancing will always remain with me. And there must be millions throughout the world who feel the same. It was an unique experience when she spoke to us with such truth, such pure imagination, and we let her lead us through the enchanted landscapes of her now legendary art.

Ekaterina Maximova

Ekaterina Maximova is that rare being, a natural soubrette who is also a great ballerina. She has the face for comedy—delicate, pretty and whimsical, with a type of jaunty insouciance, which is so beguiling, that belonged also to the two other great soubrettes, Lydia Lopokova and Renée Jeanmaire. When Dr Coppélius dreamed of his beautiful doll as a living being, one feels certain she would have looked just like Ekaterina Maximova. It is indeed disappointing that the role of Swanhilda has never been danced in London either by Maximova or Natalia Makarova, since it is extremely rare to find two ballerinas with so wide a range, and they would have much to teach dancers and audiences about true comic style in classical ballet.

However, when Maximova dances in *Giselle* or *Swan Lake*, she transforms her features into lines of tragic beauty, haunted by her wide, mysterious eyes. It is then she shapes her movements with the splendour that belongs only to the greatest ballerinas of the Russian school. Maximova has none of the affectations or blemishes of style that mar so many dancers of the Bolshoi Ballet, yet, at the same time, she has not the elegance or restrained passion of the greatest dancers of the Kirov. Her style is grand, simple and eloquent, marked by a fastidious concern for the musical line and a phenomenal technical accomplishment. It is heroic, wide in scale and noble in proportion. In a way it looks back to Trefilova and forward from Ulanova who, as her teacher, has been so great an influence on her development.

In her art we sense the great spaces of her native country, the warm and generous character of its people. I think of her as the Tolstoy of the dance, while Makarova is the Pushkin, because one can imagine the scope and wide humanity of his novels in her sweep of movement, its generosity and its repose. I think the most beautiful feature of the classical dance is this openness of movement. There is about it nothing cramped or hurried, nothing small or mean of spirit; only a spaciousness, a great calm. Maximova breathes that spirit, for her dancing is truly classical, with the same proportions, the same sense of ease. Yet it is never cold or distant; it is a human architecture, the shaping of a vital life.

Maximova has in certain respects been wasted as an artist, owing to the impoverished nature of modern Soviet choreography which lags so far behind that of the West. In her one feels a great expressive artist struggling to escape from the banalities of movement in such works as *Spartacus*, an imagination forced into narrow modes and commonplace ideas. The Bolshoi production of *Don Quixote* is quite dreadful, vulgar and silly beyond belief, yet Maximova creates something wonderful out of it, while never making the mistake of treating it seriously. She dances it for all it isn't worth. Indeed she mocks it, knowing that her audience will share the joke. She throws off staggering technical feats with impudence, even with daring, as if she challenged the music to lose all patience and thrust her from the stage. It is not just mock-Spanish; it is mockery itself, the impudence of great art trifling with the commonplace.

In *Casse-Noisette*, another dreadful production, Maximova takes a different line. She is condemned to a poor score, the worst Tchaikovsky ever wrote for the theatre, a foolish story and inexpressive choreography. She takes these elements and she transforms them, far more than could be encompassed in the foolish kingdoms of the sweets and of the snow where she is obliged to dance. She transforms them by an icy purity of classical style, set in majestic lines against the music that suddenly begins to sing in her limbs, to take on a beauty that is, in fact, only the deceptions of her art, giving to the dance and the music a new dimension they could, without her, never have achieved. It is fascinating to watch a ballerina triumph over inferior material, to see her make not just bricks without straw, but a whole palace of crystal, an architecture of daring and originality, set in splendour above the poverty of its surround.

Only in *Giselle* has Maximova been given material worthy of her. I do not feel that in the First Act she creates that sense of nervous tension and imbalance which is so important a feature of the character, but her acting and dancing have a freshness and spontaneity that bring the old story ardently alive. Here is all the innocence, the trust and the hint of an inner lack of security, that belongs to young love. The Romantic period is faultlessly reconstructed, the balance between a period drama and a true and moving story of love given and love betrayed is faultlessly maintained. Her mad-scene is lyrical and of its period, but never distant, nor yet in any sense pathological; its restraint is the measure of its grief, more moving than any realistic interpretation.

It is, however, in the Second Act that she achieves the widest range of expressiveness. Her dancing is tragic, indeed hopeless; no glimmer of that lost love remains, no hope; only a huge, elegiac grief that is expressed with an intensity, a richness of imagery, which belongs only to the greatest ballerinas. The proportions of her dancing are in themselves an architecture of grief, the tomb of a betrayed love, a monument above her grave. Here the dancing achieves the universal quality of the highest art; it speaks beyond the limits of the story or the tradition to which it belongs, for it deals with the essential sadness of death and parting, the void that lies behind an abandoned love. It is rare for classical dancing to reach the boundaries of high tragedy, but here the miracle is achieved, grief transfigured in the dance and in its repose.

Ekaterina Maximova will probably never know what powers of expression are latent within her, because she has never been given by modern Russian choreographers a real challenge to her gifts. It is sad indeed to see them wasted, to see such prodigality of art lavished on material so unworthy of it. But what she has done with it is enough to place her among the finest ballerinas of this or any other time.

Marcia Haydée

If one thinks of a bird dropping from the sky, its wings stabbing the air, ready to strike and kill, one sees in imagination Marcia Haydée pounce on a musical phrase with the same thrilling intensity, the same sweep of flight, the music a landscape spread beneath her. Or else one sees her body arched like a tightly-strung bow, ready to launch her dance on feet sharp-tipped as arrows. The controlled force of her dancing, its strength and brilliance, make her at one with the elements of earth and fire, where a world of passion smoulders in her eyes.

The first season of the Stuttgart Ballet at Covent Garden in the summer of 1974 was a personal triumph for Marcia Haydée. Her dancing in *Onegin*, *The Taming of the Shrew* and *Voluntaries* was a revelation. Of all modern choreographers, John Cranko had the most profound sense of structure in the line of the dance, both in solo work and *pas de deux*. He composed images of astonishing power, a kind of living architecture, where the line created by the dancers had an intricacy and a grandeur unmatched by his contemporaries. In Marcia Haydée he found his muse, a ballerina whose sense of proportion never deserts her, and who created for him these living statues of such amazing grace. In *adagio* her movements uncoil like an opening spring in huge arcs around her, the tension held at the point of most exact balance. Yet there is nothing cold about her dancing; this is not the style of Trefilova, a study in marbled perfection, but a living, human art throbbing with an intensity of emotion than runs through her dance, dark as blood.

In repose her body is compact with the potential of brilliant movement, for she has a kind of latent power one notices in certain animals. Watching her, I was reminded of part of a poem by Edith Sitwell that best expresses this aspect of her art:

Said the Lion to the Lioness—'When you are amber dust,—
No more a raging fire like the heat of the Sun
(No liking but all lust)—
Remember still the flowering of the amber blood and bone
The rippling of bright muscles like a sea,
Remember the rose-prickles of bright paws
Though we shall mate no more
Till the fire of that sun the heart and the moon-cold bone are one.

Here we see her dance, "the rippling of bright muscles like a sea"—its force, its proportions. In the thrust and sweep of her dancing one finds images of desperate beauty, made visible in her limbs, so that in *Onegin* they flower like the opening of a dark rose.

In *The Taming of the Shrew* she displays an entirely different aspect of her talent. Now she is prepared to mock her own style, to ape the movements of Haydée the *prima ballerina* with a flat-footed stance that would be more appropriate for an irate duck. To see her waddle across the stage, elbows stuck out, jaw at a threatening angle, her face constricted into a blank scowl, was to watch an absurd parody of herself. Yet, ridiculous though her Katherine is, at the same time she is a figure of considerable pathos; within this body, contorted with aggravation, was a lonely woman who believed herself incapable of being loved. To see her melt with such huge reluctance during her *pas de deux* with Petruchio was as pathetic as it was vastly amusing: the goose remained a goose, but one had the suspicion she had begun to believe herself a swan. The disillusionment when she found that Petruchio still intended to tame her was quite startling, since she lost faith in this new and delightful transformation, and was a goose again. This is acting and dancing of great intelligence and compassion; it moved one to laughter, but it was not so far from tears.

The revelation of the season was Glen Tetley's *Voluntaries*, a ballet about which I have written at some length earlier. I shall never forget the opening moments, danced in silence, where she stands with her arms curved high around her, like some primitive bird set in the empty sky in the chaos of the uncreated world, a phoenix rising from the ashes of a dead star to be reborn again in the flames of the music, as the first chord springs from the darkness. Seldom in modern ballet can a choreographer's vision have been so supremely understood or interpreted with such fidelity. Indeed the movements of the other dancers became echoes of her own, matching her style that dominated the entire ballet.

Marcia Haydée created the leading role in Kenneth MacMillan's *Song of the Earth*, and it is fascinating to compare this with the recent interpretation of Natalia Makarova in the same part. Makarova's dancing is a fragile meditation on the music, full of a lingering sadness. We see the beauty of all that is passing, all to be lost in the end. In Haydée's performance, there is the acceptance with her whole being of an endless dark. They dance two aspects of the same truth, two statements of the most sublime art.

I see Marcia Haydée most clearly in repose, compact of a thousand images that are ready to spring into life, when she will link them together in the wide sweep of a single statement, a great stanza of poetic dance. Then she will cross the stage as a falling star blazes in an empty sky, this great dancer of fire and the living earth.

Eva Evdokimova

Eva Evdokimova is the youngest of all modern ballerinas, though she has had an experience wider than most, exceptional indeed in one of her age. She has studied at the Munich Opera School and the Royal Ballet School, danced with the Royal Danish Ballet and the Deutsche Opera in Berlin. Most important of all, she has worked with Dudinskaya at the Kirov, thus being the only member of a British Ballet company, the Festival Ballet which she joined in 1974, who has been directly in touch with the Vaganova/Kirov style, the most perfect to be seen at the present time. She won the only gold medal at the Varna International dance competition in 1970. She is now only twenty-six years old.

I put these bare facts at the beginning, for she has time enough to absorb all she has learned and the full flowering of her talent lies in the future. Yet she is a superb ballerina already, an artist of so pure a style that she is like a ghost from the past. One sees in her the noble proportions of the dancing of Vera Trefilova, the full, rounded grace of Yvette Chauviré, the authority and sweep of movement of Galina Ulanova. She is both a summary of the past and an intimation of the future, one who inherits the tradition of the classical dance by direct descent. Even without the beauty of her own performances, it is touching to see so young a ballerina who carries the weight of such a long tradition.

Her beauty is exceptional, containing within it something of the romanticism of the young Karsavina, something of the haunted expression of Olga Spessivtzeva. Taller than most dancers, fine-drawn with a gentle, wistful face, she can invoke by one fragile smile the whole lost world of the Romantic Ballet. Her dancing flows in long lines, softer and more lyrical than must have been that of many famous ballerinas of the past, yet they have the same delicacy as those lithographs from so long ago. Her Giselle, which she studied with Chauviré, one of the finest of its modern exponents, is a perfect evocation of the Romantic age, where her rounded arms and soft movements recreate the style of the French school to which Carlotta Grisi, the first Giselle, belonged.

It is a curious thing that one is prompted to write of Evdokimova so much in terms of the past, but I think the reason for this is that so many ballerinas of former ages seem to live again in her dancing, so true is it to the traditions of the classical dance. Indeed Evdokimova, because of her varied training and experience, is a kind of summary of its history: she is the meeting point of the Italian, French, Russian and English schools, their centre of beautiful repose.

Her incredible lightness of movement brings a rare poetry to the Second Act of *Giselle*. Even when she walks or runs across the stage it appears as if the music were the magic air on which she dances. Her art is quite without sentimentality or any falseness of expression; one does not see with her those coy and sickening affectations of movement by which certain modern dancers (one in particular, whom I shall not mention) reduce the Romantic movement to a Victorian tea party. Instead we find dancing that is objective, intelligent and governed by a creative imagination, far removed from such fake romanticism. Although she cannot reach the heights of emotional expression contained in Makarova's performance, her dancing is honest, serious and richly wrought from the music, a pure classicism, an example in style and in the aristocratic traditions of the past.

Yet she is not limited to this; indeed she has the rare gift of being able to develop and change her style in accordance with the type of ballet she dances. As Odette she creates wide, spacious images, huge in their proportions, at times even perhaps too elaborate, while as Odile she dances with an icy brilliance, making even the notorious *fouettés* a part of the character, rather than a *tour de force* of considerable vulgarity.

Her Aurora is no less remarkable, for she draws an unusual portrait of a young beauty toying with the affections of her suitors whom, at the same time, she mocks to her companions secretly behind their backs. One knows she is very conscious of being a princess, though less aware, it seems, that she behaves a little like a spoilt brat. It is an interpretation of extraordinary sophistication, far removed from the expected, yet truly classical in the dance, where the poses *en attitude* are as beautiful as the unfolding of a flower.

Evdokimova has already the authority of the true ballerina, the poise, the aristocracy. She is, in some ways, unique—a pure classicist, complete apart from a few technical blemishes, schooled at the fountainhead of Russian ballet, far in advance of her contemporaries of the same age in her understanding of this tradition, an artist a little apart, yet seemingly unafraid of the responsibilities she has inherited. It is hard to see in which way she may develop. Together with Jennifer Penney, a ballerina of nearly the same age but with a less wide experience, who is the bright hope of the Royal Ballet and its most exquisite stylist, Eva Evdokimova holds most promise for the future. But there is a danger in it, for she may have developed too rapidly, in a sense outgrown her potential.

It is certainly true that Beryl Grey, the Artistic Director of the

Festival Ballet, who has in such a short period brought the Company up to an entirely different standard from the past, has a great responsibility for the future of Eva Evdokimova, this rare jewel of a dancer. One hopes that new roles will be mounted for her, so that she may test further the limits of her resources, both technical and emotional, and find in doing so that there are riches hidden there which she cannot yet enjoy. Certainly it would be sad if so exceptional a young ballerina, so perfectly schooled, were left to dance only traditional classic and romantic roles, and one hopes she may soon be allowed to abandon *The Nutcracker* and similar coloured toys that are unworthy of her. She needs a choreographer who will find in her his muse, and reveal for her and for us her true potential and all the bright treasures of her art.

Natalia Makarova

I can remember so vividly the first time I saw Natalia Makarova dance. It was in *Giselle*, her début in the title role, at Covent Garden in 1961. Even now I recall the shiver of recognition, denoting to me the presence of genius. Since that night I have watched every performance she has given in London, and during these years I became increasingly sure that she must be the greatest ballerina to appear there since Olga Spessivtzeva danced, also in *Giselle*, at the Savoy Theatre in 1932. Certainly in over thirty years of watching the ballet I have never seen her equal.

The dancing of Natalia Makarova is the greatest single achievement of the teaching ideas of Agrippina Vaganova which have developed the Russian school to the highest point of expressiveness yet attained in classical ballet, summarised now in the art of one great ballerina. Vaganova incorporated into the traditional style of the Imperial Theatre a new pliancy of movement, a freedom and a plasticity, that had been developed by Michel Fokine, in which the arms, shoulders and upper torso were given a much greater degree of flexibility, so that the whole body could speak in the imagery of the dance. It is the style now taught to the members of the Kirov School, of whom Makarova is the incomparable representative.

Quite rightly, and with the courage and artistic integrity that have marked her career, Makarova left the Kirov Ballet in 1970. Although the Company had given her a matchless training as a classical ballerina, it could offer her no scope to enrich her art on an emotional and expressive level, owing to the lack of good choreographers in the Soviet Union and the bureaucratic restrictions to which those of original talent were subjected. Her decision has been amply justified: she is now not only a greater classical ballerina, with a range far beyond that of any of her contemporaries either in the East or West, but she is also a superlative exponent of modern choreography, including the ballets of Antony Tudor and Kenneth MacMillan. It is true, of course, that she has still not been given the full range of opportunities appropriate to her genius. She has danced frequently with the American Ballet Theater and as a guest artist with many companies, and far too infrequently with the Royal Ballet which, with its unmatched repertoire of classical and modern works is, it seems to me, her true artistic home. Nevertheless she remains the supreme exemplar of the Russian school, and so must have a profound influence on the development of this style in the West.

In a sense, having described the performances of other ballerinas in the earlier pages, I have, in part, described her also, since her scope is so enormous that it has an universal quality which belongs to all great art. It has a majesty of line, a response to music so sensitive that the music is like the song of her own body when she dances, an emotional force that, in dramatic roles, blazes on the stage like an explosion of stars. To this is added a lyrical style, sublimely evocative of the Romantic Ballet, a classical technique of amazing splendour. She is at home equally in the ballets of the nineteenth century as she is in those of our own time; in her dancing two centuries meet, and magically they are reconciled.

To watch Makarova phrase a classical *variation* is to observe a great theatrical intelligence and imagination brought to bear on its material with the same fastidious concern for detail as that shown by a painter or a sculptor. The steps of the dance are her raw material which she shapes in accordance with their nature, showing them, by the most subtle combination of stress, dynamics and delicacy of musical thought, in an entirely new light. It is dancing that is truly creative—a private vision, contained in music, drawn with delicate precision on the air. In the closing minutes of *Song of the Earth*, for example, she can be seen to shape the music with her arms, as it must have first formed itself in the composer's mind, sung to him out of his own silence.

She has also an ability to create the atmosphere of any ballet she dances, so that she moves as if behind a transparent veil cast by the music, not only drawing it in line but also recreating it in colour. In the Second Act of *Giselle* and in *Les Sylphides* she glimmers, moth-like, through its shadowed world, creature of the night, of the mysterious dark. Her relationship to the music is like that of a bird's song that might thread itself, like a string of beads, to the night wind. It is her own dark wood from which she glides on a shimmer of translucent wings, turning, half-dazed, in the light of the moon. In *Les Sylphides* she has come from another world; between herself and the Poet there is no true communion, even when she turns and looks at him in the *adagio* with a glance that is both shy and secretive, mocked by the ghost of a smile. She will never disclose to him from whence she came: this is a knowledge she shares only with the music that companions her always, even beyond the far stars.

The greatest dancers will excel not only in the major works of the classical repertoire, but also in miniatures where a compression of images and emotional intensity is the essential feature. Pavlova triumphed in such a way, making her small solos, particularly *The Dying Swan*, sublime allegories of the human spirit, poems that carried within them huge echoes and resonances. One is, perhaps, closer to the ballerina in such works, closer to the essence of her art, than in her major roles; through them her inner nature is most surely revealed. The same is true of Natalia Makarova when one sees her in the tiny *pas de deux* called *Spring Waters*, danced to the music of Rachmaninov.

Here is all the rush of Spring—the torrents of green water, set free from the melting snows, the tremor of the first leaves, the stems of the daffodils before the flowers have opened. So brief, such a flash of light, the dancers are like two kingfishers, dipping in the air, swooping between the trees. It is a sudden ecstatic flight, carried upwards on the wings of music. One is reminded by her of a wave about to break, curved and silver-tipped, poised above the sea. She does not dance to the music, rather is she swept along by it; it flings her upwards, holds her in one ecstatic pose, spins her as if caught in the whirlpool. Here the dance is elemental, a force of nature; it belongs in all its iridescence, its shimmering light, to the great Spring rains that set the river thundering between its banks, flooding the fields. It is free in all the daring, all the sudden improvisations of the Spring.

Her dance reflects the music, as a river mirrors the sky above it, carries at night the stars.

One feels the sense of a great expanse of earth and air, a huge landscape wheeling away into the distance. It is Spring in Russia, not the delicate prettiness of our own country, but the wide green cornfields, the apple orchards, the shapes of trees drawn against the horizon. In some strange way this dance, brief though it is, must seem to her like the memory of her own land to which she may never be able to return. It is her gift to us, her evocation of that mysterious country, so real to her, so far from our own. Her dancing here reminds me of some of the scene painting in the novels of Turgenev—a world remembered in exile, loved for its solitude, the silence of its empty spaces, the stillness out of time.

In a different manner she achieves an equally startling effect with the absurd *pas de deux* from *Don Quixote*, the old war-horse that is trundled out for gala performances to cavort once again on its circus-legs and prove that it can still go through its paces. Here she dances with all the panache of a plume on the head of a circus pony, as light, as free, equally nonchalant. It is a joke that must be shared by the audience, bombarded by a fusillade of smiles, drawn into the act with a merry complicity, a kind of casual daring. The ferocious balances are held just a little longer than is seemly, then dismissed with a little twirl of the hands as wholly irrelevant, a kind of frivolity with which she indulges

F

herself, having the time to spare. We are vamped quite out-rageously over the top of a fan, or given side-long glances that mock our solemnity as we sit there in rows like a congregation in church, a little put out by the levity of the parson. Yet as this scarlet flame flickers on the stage, we begin to realise that this is not just an act of impossible daring; it is a kind of free cadenza, exquisite and ornate, that has been built out of the music to an architecture of her own devising. The circus has become a work of art.

We often think of the ballerina in terms of the tragic roles she so often plays, yet we sometimes forget the many facets of happiness that she is able to express. There is happiness, grasped so uncertainly, haunted by the threat of darkness, in *Giselle*—the play of light and shade, the sudden chill in the air at the end of autumn; there is joy expressed in terms of physical sensation as in *Romeo and Juliet*; there is the mischievous, inventive delight of Swanhilda, the spoilt brat of *Coppélia*, all bluff and bravado; or joy that comes like a gift, the confirmation of a hope so long delayed as in *Cinderella*; the immature happiness, so perilous and so full of adventure, in *The Sleeping Beauty* where, in the final Act, we see that joy mature in the fullness of an adult love—of all these she is the true chronicler: of youth and love, even of the treacherous promise of spring-time. When we "hold a mirror up to nature" we can see, reflected in it, her dance.

Perhaps Makarova's greatest achievement to date is her performance in Kenneth MacMillan's *Romeo and Juliet*, about which I wrote in some detail in my earlier book, *The Ballerina*. Here the fusion between the poetry, the music and the images of the dance is achieved in one sweep of her creative imagina-tion, so that it becomes a profound study in the nature of human love, the dignity and the grief of human passion.

If one chooses three dances—those for the ballerina in the ballroom scene, beneath the balcony and in the final *pas de deux* with Paris—one can see how Makarova reconciles the choreo-graphy with the inner logic of the music's design. The solo in the ballroom scene is shaped around music that is brilliant in outline as if it had been drawn on glass in diamond point. When she dances, each step is formed as if it had been cut out of the icy air, with a kind of frosted brilliance. The dance reaches with the music to sudden climaxes for which we are not prepared, a design of dazzling fragments, intricate as a mosaic. It is jewelled dancing, clear as the fire that glitters above a string of diamonds.

In the balcony scene the music is lit by moonlight, full of the sounds and scents of a summer night. Her heart throbs from within it, pulses to the rhythm of her blood. Here the dance ripples and shimmers like the tide that turns beneath the moon. It is enchanted, where the surrender to love is complete, and there is no reason, no logic in it any more. It is ecstatic, a kind of madness. All the abandonment of love is in her dancing, the obliteration of self in a moment's total surrender, the daring that will risk all in one final utterance.

The last *pas de deux* with Paris is a duet faint from a mortal sickness; in it is a sense of revulsion from which the defeated spirit turns, shuddering and afraid. Now her body faints, sinks into a final surrender; it is bereft of life, of vital movement, of any hope. Now she expresses a misery that has not even the will to despair, a kind of hideous echo of all that she has danced before, all the hopes now defaced, the love disfigured, and the shame.

There is a profound irony in that the music here, from the moment of the entry of Juliet's parents with Paris, is a re-capitulation of part of the music from the joyous ballroom scene. Juliet's *pas de deux* with Paris is a sad echo of the same dance then, even to the gesture of her arms, reaching upwards, that is linked to the same little curling phrase in the music, but now her body droops most piteously, and the gesture is no longer one of happiness but despair.

I remember, and see them now, those moments of stillness, perfect in line, emotion sculptured in a single pose: the moment when she first greets Romeo, her eyes, huge and awakening with love; the moment when he leaves her after their bridal night, and she is alone on the empty stage—a pose that in an instant accepts all, wills all the consequences of her loving; when her father flings her to the ground after her rejection of Paris, and she reaches in despair to the empty bed, then turns her face away, her arms limp at her sides. I remember her in flight to

Friar Laurence, her cloak, flame-like, fluttering behind her; or beneath the balcony, moving across the stage like rippling water. I see her now in the first scene—the wide leaps, the little runs on *points* when she is suddenly so secretive and alone, and which we are to see again when she breaks free from Paris, chooses her own solitude, her unspoken despair.

All the stages of human love are in this performance. Her arms speak; her body is a chorus of voices.

Her dancing in the classic ballets of the nineteenth century sets a standard unlikely to be reached in our time. It has purity of execution, beauty of musical phrasing, and a depth of characterisation that are co-ordinated by an understanding of the ballet as a whole and the relationship of its parts, that are uniquely her own. Here form and content become one in a statement of absolute beauty. I am amazed by the manner in which she establishes the mood of the ballet and the character of its heroine from the moment she takes the stage: this is the truth of Odette or Aurora or Giselle, made visible in the dance by sudden flashes of insight into the very depths of the music where it resides.

Here is Giselle—a girl who grasps at a hope in which she does not believe, a pledge that even as she gives it, she knows will be betrayed. At first she is like a small wild creature that has crept into the light, vulnerable and alone, trusting so much and so little, and so afraid. She is disturbed by each faint tremor in the music that is like a shiver of recognition, the knowledge sought for in an unspoken question, a game with flowers. It is a dream of love that has enchanted her, and it is only the truth she cannot face that would keep her sane. One can see it in the way she will not, at first, meet Albrecht's eyes. It is in part modesty, for she does not wish him to see the love she cannot hide; but it is also fear that she might discern the first hint of betrayal in his own. In the same way, plucking the petals from a flower, she freezes, suddenly immobile, seeing the truth there, and knowing then a presentiment too terrible for her reason to bear.

Her solos in the First Act are like brush-strokes touched on the surface of the air, delicate in their fragility as the painter might set the first leaves against the sky. This dancing is an enchanted landscape, lit by music which is its own light. She turns so slowly, holding a perfect balance, like a leaf coiled in the wind. It is a painting by Corot, her arms the thin branches of winter trees.

The scene of madness compresses, in a few distorted minutes, all that has gone before: her meeting with Albrecht, the dance he taught her—so tragic now in its broken lines, like the anguished stabs of memory. She turns with her twisted hands the stems of those prophetic flowers; she reaches now for a kiss, searches blindly with groping arms the empty air. It has in her choice of moments to remember all the terrible logic, the cruel insight of the insane.

In the Second Act she moves, distant and luminous in the hazy light of the music, like the glimmer of the hidden moon, a troubled dream to haunt Albrecht's imagination in the darkness of his grieving. He grasps at this shadow, impalpable as air or the night winds on which she is floating. Here the dancing becomes a great elegy of human love, eternal beyond the grave. Here the classical style is transcended: the dance, the music and the dancer are one in a single statement of imperious art.

Makarova is a truly creative artist, never satisfied with her achievements, in search always for the impossible ideal. Continually she makes alterations both in style and detail to her performances of traditional roles, seeking from them greater expressiveness in the classical style. When she returned to dance Odette/Odile with the Royal Ballet in November 1974, one could see how much her interpretation had developed. Her dancing in the Second Act was now built in great harmonies, with a kind of orchestral richness of movement. Each phrase grew to its own huge proportions, so that the effect was like a series of arches leading to the most distant perspective, the apotheosis of the classical style expressed in terms of elegy. From her first entry, when she appeared to settle on throbbing wings in a single sweep of flight, to her last sad *bourrées*, we were swept up into a world of enchantment that she had discovered in the music, where the myth was expressed with all the tragic intensity of her art. The immense landscape that lies

165

F*

beyond the classical dance was spread out before us, enclosed, as if by the curve of two rivers, in the line of her wonderous arms. Verlaine describes the essence of her art in four lines:

> Votre âme est un paysage choisi
> Que vont charmant masques et bergamasques
> Jouant du luth et dansant et quais
> Tristes sous leurs déguisements fantasques.

Makarova had also clearly re-thought the choreography of the Third Act and the relationship between Odile and Sigfried. Normally the ballerina will seek only to dazzle; with Makarova there was this, but also a sense of extraordinary malignancy in which she held Sigfried transfixed as if in a hypnotic trance. Never did she relent, nor abjure her power over him that seemed conjured out of the air by black magic and secret rites. Her Odette was not a person: she was a spirit of evil, invoked by necromancy. In her *équilibres* she held her body arched and tense like a serpent about to strike; her dancing so brilliant, sharp-edged and cold, glittered like a sunlight over ice, diamond-pointed, a flash in the jewelled air.

Makarova has an extraordinary insight into the ballets of Kenneth MacMillan, proved first by her performance in *Romeo and Juliet*, and confirmed by the title role in *Manon* which she danced at Covent Garden in November 1974. As a choreographer MacMillan was himself profoundly influenced by the dancing of Lynn Seymour, upon whom he mounted many of his works, giving them their character of plasticity of movement, sweep and intensity of expression, that were her own, very different indeed from the other neat, restrained stylists of the Royal Ballet. In Makarova he found these qualities again, now magnified and extended by the Kirov schooling, to which she has added her own poetic insight into the nature of the role.

From her first entry Makarova at once establishes the character of Manon—the precocious coquette, at once both innocent and knowing, already conscious of her power to charm, to win rich hearts; a girl who is only seventeen, yet is already wise in the handling of men, not knowing how vulnerable she may be herself. Manon is greedy, selfish, an expensive flirt, but in

Makarova's interpretation there is always retained a sense of innocence, a heart too light, too easily swayed. To watch her reject an elderly admirer with such delicacy, softening the rebuke by tickling him under the chin, or see her draw greedily forwards to touch a woman's jewelled necklace, or brush aside a compliment with a lowering of her modest and all-observant eyes, is to know great dramatic acting, achieved by the smallest touches of observation. Extraordinary, too, is how, seated on a chair, she becomes one with des Grieux in his first impassioned solo; here, by altering the angle of her head and body, with tiny gestures and shifts of movement, she expresses a whole range of emotions from curiosity to sexual attraction and growing love, superbly related to the music and the changing moods of the male solo.

In the party scene her own *variation* is danced with a kind of sensuality and exotic beauty that indicates how Manon has found her destiny as a high-class courtesan. At the same time the child lives on behind this veneer of sophistication, smiles at her lover over a fan. Imperious to the servants, at once both haughty and beguiling to her admirers, easily bored, easily amused, she remains not only a depraved child but also hints at a woman capable of suffering and genuine love. As in all Makarova's interpretations, the character is seen whole, not only in act but also in potential, through this extraordinary creative intuition that is her unique characteristic as a dramatic ballerina.

In the four superb *pas de deux* round which the work is built, Makarova encompasses a world of love, from flirtatiousness to tragic submission. In the last of these, majestically partnered by Anthony Dowell, her dancing is lit by an unearthly radiance; all the self-love is dead now, the greed and the wilfulness; the light is spent. She moves, unwilled, through the music, where only the ghost of her impetuous spirit remains, purified as if within purgatorial fires. Here Makarova sublimates the classical dance to express a profound moral truth: in love and expiation, even in her dying moments, Manon fulfills her destiny. The imprisoned spirit, no longer bound by her fiickle body, speaks to us in images beyond the power of words.

Genius is a far country, and to follow Makarova there is to attempt to describe the topography of an unknown land. Lit by its unearthly light, this last scene of *Manon* is a glimpse of that secret world she inhabits, where the spirit is unfettered, and lives on, free and immortal, in these great statements of a classic art.

Immediately following her engagement with the Royal Ballet in November 1974, Makarova appeared in Copenhagen, partnered by Mikhail Barishnikov, in *La Sylphide* with the Royal Danish Ballet. The gilded proscenium of the Theatre Royal became, as she danced, the frame for a series of lithographs, etched by her with an exquisite precision, so that the old ballet of the nineteenth century lived again, unspoiled and intact, in its true home.

Makarova's Sylphide was half spirit, half child, wilful, impetuous and sly, full of sweet mockery, tenderness and guile. To watch her in the First Act indicate to James her falling tears was to find a perfect balance between Victorian sentiment and true grief, as touching and poignant as music from a spinet or a harpsichord. Here was all the sweet romance of a Valentine, now decorated by appropriate tears, a world of loving sighs. It was not pastiche but recreation, a lost world recalled in her huge sad eyes.

In the Second Act her dancing opened to the music as some mysterious night-flower, the symbol of her art, might open to the moon. I shall always remember how in one solo two single turns *en attitude* formed themselves with a kind of piercing beauty, pale and translucent like an arctic rose. The air supported her, this stranger to our mortal earth.

Makarova's dancing was so intricately woven from the music that it seemed to be embroidered from it, each musical phrase a silken thread. The resultant picture was like a Victorian keepsake, so pretty, so delicate in outline, that it belonged to an age far distant from our own. Her sense of period was impeccable; this portrait became a sublime evocation of Lucile Grahn, the first Sylphide at the Theatre Royal nearly a hundred and fifty years ago, whom the critic Jules Janin described as "a beautiful person who dances like the singing of a bird".

Few scenes in contemporary ballet can be so moving as the death of this Sylphide—her taut, stricken body, arched in a mortal anguish; the shudder of her last expiring sigh; the emptiness of her eyes that were once the harbingers of such beauty and such high romance. It was a moment of extraordinary pathos: it seemed as if a child had died, the merry and beguiling spirit with her mocking eyes, now no more substantial than a blossom drifting to the earth.

If one considers Natalia Makarova's evocations of the Romantic Ballet, it is amazing to see how widely they differ. In *Les Sylphides* she does not belong to this earth, for she listens to echoes from far away, voices calling to her from the skies, to which soon she will return, where she truly abides. Memories haunt her within each musical phrase, so that one is reminded of the superb lines from Guillaume Apollinaire:

> Les souvenirs sont cors de chasse
> dont meurt le bruit parmi le vent.

In *Giselle* her dancing is huge in its sweep, elegiac in its phrasing, a tragic statement of loneliness and transfigured love. Here one sees a love remembered in that exile "from whose bourn no traveller returns"; it is the darkness at the end of the long bright day, a grief that is human, yet now without substance of a living heart. In *La Sylphide* her interpretation is like the flirtation of a spirit with a human love, the coquetry of a selfish child, wilful and uncaring, yet not truly of this earth. She is part of the night's enchantment, a glimpse of the ideal, set between sleep and waking.

With these recent performances in London and Copenhagen, Natalia Makarova has reached the last frontier of her art: ahead of her lies an unknown country which she must explore alone, guided only by the light of her genius. Nothing now is beyond her, either technically or emotionally, no summit too high, no river too broad for her to cross. Perhaps of all other ballerinas, only Anne Pavlova knew the way in this strange land, and its secrets are buried with her.

One hopes that modern choreographers will recognise the sublime instrument that is available to them, and create roles for Natalia Makarova worthy of her gifts. Her dancing is an invitation and it is also a challenge; one trusts that they will have the courage to accept it and bring to light all those sleeping images that can be awakened only by her art.

These performances of hers are allegories of the human spirit, enigmatic and all-knowing like our dreams. There is no end to them, no certain discovery; only mysteries opening one onto another like doors to secret rooms. This art, with its huge disciplines, contains her, yet the freedom she finds within it is one she has discovered alone; it is beyond imitation, for it comes, like an Ariel, only at her bidding. The mystery of genius is that we feel at any moment we may discover it but we grasp the empty air; it is a phantom that will always elude us, even as, almost mockingly, it invites us to search for it anew. Again and again I reach for it in words—to describe that which speaks to her in music, whose design she shapes with such sublime logic on the air. In the end I am left with nothing—the tatters of a few empty phrases, sentences that form themselves around a void. My words cannot contain her; they trail away on a row of dots like a defeated sigh . . .

To describe the summit of an art when this has been attained is no easy task for a writer, for it is a place full of mystery, the dark side of the moon. It is lonely there, the solitude of genius. Natalia Makarova cannot be unaware of her stupendous talent; she is too dedicated and scrupulous an artist for that, but I think sometimes it must make her uneasy, make her afraid, conscious of the demands it forces upon her, this restless spirit that can never be conquered, never wholly assuaged. Yet of one thing at least I am certain: in her the dance finds its fulfilment, its immortal repose.

Epilogue

The bright dancers are gone. The stage is empty. We are left only with memories. The future belongs to the young dancers who have helped to illustrate this book, and to so many like them across the world. It is theirs by right. They have their inheritance.

French Texts

Page 63

Ici la fusion de l'être organique et de la forme abstraite est miraculeusement accomplie. La danseuse s'ouvre comme une fleur; elle n'est même plus une femme; plus près de la nature qu'un être humain, elle respire comme une plante qui exhalerait son parfum. Et voilà qu'elle devient, le mouvement exécuté, un symbole abstrait érigé par l'intelligence. Ou bien elle s'élance et s'envole, libellule, papillon, cygne—autant de symboles d'une animalité radieuse et ailée—pour devenir, en achevant son enchaînement, équilibre, éternité, statue, simulacre de l'immuable beauté. A tout moment, la danseuse oscillant entre l'instinct profond et la géométrie dans l'espace réalise ce que notre ami, André Lhote appela 'l'utilisation plastique du coup de foudre.'

Page 117

Mais toujours ils allaient chercher leur inspiration *en dehors* de la danse, prise en soi. Toujours—et c'est le vice initial de leur esthétique—ils la déforment, la torturent, l'adaptent à l'expression de quelque chose d'autre qui lui est étranger. Jamais elle ne s'épanouit librement, indépendamment de tout pastiche et de toute parodie, 'acte pur des métamorphoses', comme eût dit M. Paul Valéry.

Nous croyons avoir formulé notre principale objection contre la manière de voir et la façon d'agir des Ballets Russes à toutes les époques successives de leur triomphe at de leur déclin. En frustrant la danse de son autonomie et en l'incorporant à un spectacle ingénieux mais composite, hybride, inorganique, les dirigeants de la célèbre troupe l'ont vouée au caprice du jour et aboli la continuité d'une culture chorégraphique qui est une des expressions suprêmes du génie occidental.

Page 133

. . . il y a beaucoup de danseuses même mediocres qui s'ingénient à emporter de haute lutte telle difficulté ou à réussir par hasard un temps très brillant. Or, ce qui leur manquera toujours c'est la cohésion parfaite des enchaînements, le développement du mouvement qui n'admet pas de lacunes et qui fait d'un pas de Trefilova ce que Wagner appela, en musique, la mélodie continue.

Dans les temps d'adage, le jeu des courbes et des verticales est d'une pureté sans pareille; elle se 'développe' comme une corolle qui s'ouvre. Et ses ports de bras paraissent, telle est la précision élégante des contours, circonscrits par le crayon d'Ingres, depuis le regard rayonnant jusqu'aux pointes. Les bonds vertigineux ne sont pas faits pour elle, ni les grandes effusions passionnées. Pavlova est l'oiseau: elle est la fleur. Instrument admirable qui serait en même temps le musicien: Stradivarius dansant.

Aucune saccade ne bouscule cette cantilène des lignes, aucune hésitation ne la désagrège; et c'est ce *legato* merveilleux qui fait de la danse de Trefilova un langage de formes articulé. Car nous sommes loin avec elle de ces exclamations entrecoupées ou de ce hoquet intermittent qui, emprunté au vocabulaire de la danse, parvient à donner le change à une partie du public.

Page 137

La suavité de son charme physique, sa face d'héroïne byronienne échappée d'un keepsake, équivalent à la subtilité de son intelligence cultivée. Les autres grandes Russes sont d'admirables instinctives. L'esprit de la danse d'école, la loi esthétique qui la régit, sont devinés par leur intuition. L'effort de Karsavina est conscient. Elle reconnaît les éléments que lui fournit l'école et les utilise selon son entendement. Ainsi, elle réalise un art composite et délicat . . . Spectre ou ondine, âme en peine ou libellule, Karsavina ne dépouille jamais son exquise féminité, douloureuse ou souriante. Elle anima de cette féminité la plupart des créations de Fokine; elle se dévoua à la pensée de ce maître, au détriment même de sa propre 'forme' technique, et, par la qualité de sa nature, conféra une rare noblesse à telles de ses figures qui côtoyaient la vulgarité. . . .

Page 140

Le 'phénomene Pavlova' résulte de la providentielle rencontre entre une manière d'être personnelle et les données d'un style, entre une sensibilité prodigieusement vivante et un ensemble de formes élaboré et selectionné à travers les siècles. Pavlova ranime et dépasse une tradition. Ce qu'il y a dans notre sentiment de la beauté de permanent, d'inaltérable, d'universellement, valable—l'algèbre des proportions, les lois de l'équilibre et de l'alternance,—se manifeste spontanément dans chaque portement du corps, tour ou bond de cette jeune femme qui fait des pointes sur le plateau d'un théâtre. Car il se trouve que chacun de ses gestes est l'expression-type, le signe le plus éloquent de ce que nous portons en nous. Son air est l'expression la plus personnelle des choses les plus générales. Il est de notre temps, mais aussi de tous les temps . . . Sa danse concilie l'instinct obscur et l'abstraction lucide. C'est un métal en fusion qui se déverse dans un moule et devient statue. Pavlova possède le double don de couler toute émotion dans une forme et de saturer toute forme d'émotion. Elle est la plus passionnée des danseuses et la plus harmoniouse des mimes. Et cette exubérance exquise de l'être, cette joie et cette douleur de vivre qui débordent les tracés d'un art rigoureusement abstrait expliquent la fascination qu' exerce l'insigne étoile russe. Pavlova dansant une variation classique est pareille à une flamme qui nous apparaît à travers des parois de cristal.

Page 143

C'est un être singulier et unique, tant il est conforme à certain type de beauté chorégraphique, celui créé par Taglioni. Même les linéaments allongés et vibrants de Spessivtzeva, sa forme humaine idéalisée à l'extrême, exagèrent, s'il se peut, la conformation de la séraphique Sylphide. La délicatesse, la fragilité touchante de la nouvelle Giselle vont jusqu'à paraître maladives. Mais 'la morbidezza' est, pour cette élégiaque, un attrait de plus. Le dessin des jambes, le contour du cou-de-pied sont admirables. Une simple préparation à la quatrième se revêt, avec de telles jambes, d'une beauté très rare. Le corps de Spessivtzeva aurait été digne d'être habité par le génie. Il l'est par un esprit étrange, douloureux, fatigué, résigné, quelquefois comme absent. Rien de l'ouragan de l'âme qui souffle sur Pavlova. Celle-ci est comme un lis étincelant en sa candeur. Spessivtzeva, songeuse et meurtrie, la tête penchée, les épaules un peu courbées, n'est-elle pas plutôt le saule cher aux vingt ans mélancoliques de Musset?

Or, cette suave convalescente est une danseuse de la plus grande envergure et d'une science peu commune. Ses longues jambes effilées dégagent avec une splendide ampleur. Elles servent de ressorts à des temps sautés, enlevés à une belle hauteur. La pointe si fine porte avec aisance le poids du corps dans des relevés qui soulèvent une trombe d'applaudissements. Et l'arabesque penchée de l'étoile vibre longuement comme la corde d'un Amati . . . Cette femme est—s'il est permis de modifier un texte célèbre—un roseau dansant.

Bibliography

(Note: *This is not in any sense a full bibliography of books on dancing, but relates solely to those I have consulted, however briefly, in writing this study. R.A.*)

ARMSTRONG, EDWARD. *The Folklore of Birds* (Dover Publications, 1970)

BACKMAN, E. LOUIS. *Religious Dances* (George Allen & Unwin, 1952)

BEAUMONT, C. W. *The Ballet called Swan Lake* (Beaumont, 1952)

— *The Ballet called Giselle* (Beaumont, 1944)

— *The Diaghilev Ballet in London* (Putman, 1940)

— *Michal Fokine and his Ballets* (Beaumont, 1935)

BREMOND, HENRI. *Prayer and Poetry* (Burns Oates & Washbourne, 1927)

BUCKLEY, VINCENT. *Poetry and the Sacred* (Chatto & Windus, 1968)

CHUJOY, ANATOLE. *The New York City Ballet* (A. Knopf, 1953)

DAVY, CHARLES. *Words in the Mind* (Chatto & Windus, 1965)

DAY-LEWIS, CECIL. *The Poetic Image* (Cape, 1940)

ELIOT, T. S. *Collected Poems* (Faber, 1963)

EVANS, EDWIN. *Music and the Dance* (H. Jenkins, 1948)

FIELDER, LESLIE. *No! In thunder* (Eyre & Spottiswoode, 1963)

FRANKS, A. H. *Social Dance: A Short History* (Routledge & Kegan Paul, 1963)

— *Twentieth Century Ballet* (Burke, 1954)

GUEST, IVOR. *The Romantic Ballet in Paris* (Pitman, 1966)

— *A Dancer's Heritage* (The Dancing Times, 1960)

HALL, FERNAU. *Modern English Ballet* (Andrew Melrose, 1950)

— *An Anatomy of Ballet* (Andrew Melrose, 1953)

HASKELL, ARNOLD. *Balletomania* (Gollancz, 1934)

— *What is a Ballet?* (Macdonald, 1965)

— *Vera Trefilova* (British Continental Press, 1928)
— *Tamara Karsavina* (British Continental Press, 1930)
HONIG, E. *The Dark Conceit* (O.U.P., 1960)
HUISINGA, JOHN. *Homo Ludens* (Temple Smith, 1971)
INCE, W. N. *The Poetic Theory of Paul Valéry* (Leicester U.P., 1961)
KERENSKY, OLEG. *Ballet Scene* (Hamish Hamilton, 1970)
LAWSON, JOAN. *A History of Ballet and its Makers* (Pitman, 1964)
LEVINSON, ANDRÉ. *La Danse d'Aujourd'hui* (Paris, 1929)
LEWIS, C. S. *The Allegory of Love* (O.U.P., 1936)
LIEVEN, PRINCE P. *The Birth of Ballets-Russes* (Allen and Unwin, 1936)
LIFAR, SERGE. *The Three Graces* (Cassell, 1959)
— *Ballet: Traditional to Modern* (Putnam, 1938)
MACNEICE, LOUIS. *Variations of Parable* (Cambridge U.P., 1965)
MARTIN, JOHN. *Introduction to the Dance* (W. W. Norton, 1939)
NOVERRE, J. G., trs. BEAUMONT, C. W. *Letters on Dancing* (Beaumont, 1930)
PRAZ, MARIO. *The Romantic Agony* (O.U.P., 1933)
PRIDDIN, DEIRDRE. *The Art of Dance in French Literature* (A. & C. Black, 1952)
REYNA, FERDINANDO. *A Concise History of Ballet* (Thames & Hudson, 1965)
ROSLAVLEVA, NATALIA. *Era of the Russian Ballet* (Gollancz, 1966)
SITWELL, EDITH. *The Canticle of the Rose* (Macmillan, 1949)
SITWELL, OSBERT. *Great Morning* (Macmillan, 1948)
— *Laughter in the Next Room* (Macmillan, 1949)
SPENCE, LEWIS. *An Introduction to Mythology* (Moffat Yard, 1920)
— *Myth and Ritual in Dance, Game and Rhyme* (Walls, 1947)
STORR, ANTHONY. *The Dynamics of Creation* (Secker & Warburg, 1972)
VALÉRY, PAUL. *The Art of Poetry* (Routledge & Kegan Paul, 1958)
— *L'Ame et La Danse* (Paris, 1923)
— *Degas. Danse, Dessin* (Paris, 1965)

General Index

Index of Ballets